VERM NT

ART OF THE STATE

ART OF THE STATE

VERMONT

The Spirit of America

Text by Suzanne Mantell

Harry N. Abrams, Inc., Publishers

NEW YORK

This book was prepared for publication at
Walking Stick Press, San Francisco

Project staff:
    Series Designer: Linda Herman
    Series Editor: Diana Landau

For Harry N. Abrams, Inc.:
    Series Editor: Ruth A. Peltason

Page 1: *A Beautiful Dream: An Old Theatre Organ* (detail) by Gayleen Aiken, 1982.
    Private collection. Photo Michael Gray

Page 2: *Apple Tree Surrounded by Maples* (detail) by Wolf Kahn, 1996.
    The artist was the 1998 recipient of the Vermont Council of Art's
    Lifetime Achievement Award. *Courtesy the artist*

Library of Congress Cataloguing-in-Publication Data

Mantell, Suzanne.
    Vermont : the spirit of America, state by state / text by Suzanne Mantell.
        p.   cm. — (Art of the state)
    ISBN 0–8109–5556–3 (hardcover)
    1. Vermont—Civilization—Pictorial works.   I. Title.
    II. Series.
F50.M3   1998
974.3—dc21   98–3999

Harry N. Abrams, Inc.
100 Fifth Avenue
New York, N.Y. 10011
www.abramsbooks.com

Gathering Christmas Berries by Lee Hull, 1978. *Courtesy the artist*

CONTENTS

Grandma Moses

6c U.S. Postage

"Vermont is every American's second home."

Bernard De Voto

Vermont may be small in size and population—43rd in area, with only 59 people per square mile—but it looms large in the national imagination. To generations of Americans, Vermont has represented an unhurried rural lifestyle, a proudly independent spirit, and a close-knit sense of community. The state's scenic beauties—rugged mountains, blazing autumn foliage, snowy mountainscapes—are enshrined in calendars across the land. Its towns and villages remind us of an earlier, preindustrial America. Vermont's cultural heroes include such American archetypes as Ethan Allen, Grandma Moses, "Silent Cal" Coolidge, and Robert Frost.

Yet Vermont cannot easily be reduced to a series of postcard vistas and maple-syrupy homilies. Since its beginnings as land wrested from neighboring New Hampshire and New York, Vermont has struggled for its identity, not to mention its economic existence. The rocky land and harsh winters— "hard living in a hard place," as one chronicler put it—tested the most determined settlers. Its claim to statehood rejected at first, Vermont is among a handful of states that was once an independent republic; it existed for 14 years under its own flag. Poor roads kept it isolated, even from the rest of New England, for decades. As a result, the granite and marble that underlie Vermont's soft green hills have found their way into the character of its people: "Hit a man with an ax," says journalist John Gunther, "he will practically chip off like a block of stone."

View Along the Connecticut River, Showing Windsor, Vermont, and Mt. Ascutney by Nicolino Calyo, 1850.
Shelburne Museum

Perhaps because it had to reach deep to survive, Vermont grew long, stubborn roots that quietly sustained many of America's cherished traditions: the town meeting, the country store, the church supper, the county fair. Its heritage of open discourse and egalitarianism accommodated dozens of religious groups and nurtured influential educators like John Dewey, political leaders like Coolidge, visionaries like Brigham Young, and "green revolutionaries" like Ernst Schumacher. Innovators by the score met the challenges of

Vermont living with remarkable inventions, from the coffee percolator to superior woodburning stoves. And architecture thrived in both public and private spheres, abetted by the state's rich resources of building stone.

In many ways a link to the past, Vermont also has been providentially farsighted. The state's first public library was founded in 1791. A hundred years before the Civil War, Vermont banned slavery within its borders. The movement for free higher education gained impetus from the efforts of a Vermont senator to put aside land for public colleges. In later years Vermont became the first state to limit any proposal or development that might harm the environment. George Perkins Marsh, the country's first conservationist, was a Vermonter.

Vermont's most noteworthy creation, though, has been the industry based on its own image. Beginning in the mid-19th century and continuing to the present, Vermont has used its extraordinary scenery as a magnet to draw leisure-starved urbanites from throughout the East Coast and beyond. The white-gabled farmhouses set against contoured fields, the village greens with their tall-spired churches, the flaming sugar maples, the reliably snowy ski slopes—all were transformed into seductive and successful marketing campaigns. "Vermont Beautiful," as one early slogan called it, promised year-round pleasures—bicycling, leaf-peeping, tobogganing, skiing—affordable to ordinary folks yearning for a pastoral escape.

Handmade wooden cutter (a light sleigh). Maker unknown, c. 1840. *Shelburne Museum. Photo Ken Burris. Opposite:* Jennie Farm, near Woodstock. *Photo Al Keuning/Panoramic Images*

Not surprisingly, "outlander" artists and writers were quick to follow. Many came for a seasonal workshop or tenure at Bennington or Middlebury colleges, the Breadloaf Writers Conference, or the Marlboro Music Festival. Some took up more-or-less permanent residence: Sinclair Lewis, Pearl Buck, Alexander Solzhenitsyn, and E. Annie Proulx head a long and impressive list. Since the 1950s fine crafts such as woodworking and weaving have also thrived; annual craft fairs and an official state craft center encourage the use of indigenous materials to create objects both practical and beautiful. Vermont's arts can be enjoyed on the walls of superb small museums, in lively festivals and historic buildings, in the artists' rural studios or galleries in town.

Today the myth and reality of Vermont coexist in remarkable harmony. Unlike other places where the development juggernaut has followed the tourism trail, Vermont has stubbornly and successfully defended its natural capital; Robert Frost's description of Vermont as "a State in a natural state," if not wholly accurate, comes close. At the same time, Vermont has found its own ways of embracing the best of contemporary culture, from high-tech, low-impact mini-industry to new/old styles of agriculture based on traditional ingenuity and love of the land. The innovations that take root are shaped and nourished by the wellspring of Vermont's treasured past. ✤

VERMONT

"Green Mountain State"
14th State

Date of Statehood
MARCH 14, 1791

Capital
MONTPELIER

Bird
HERMIT THRUSH

Flower
RED CLOVER

Tree
SUGAR MAPLE

Animal
MORGAN HORSE

Insect
HONEY BEE

Soil
TUNBRIDGE SOIL SERIES

Rock
MARBLE, GRANITE,
AND SLATE

The Green Mountain State proclaims itself officially and unequivocally as lush and verdant. Its Tunbridge "sugarbush" soil purportedly makes Vermont's hills greener than those in nearby New York or New Hampshire, and was designated the state soil over 160 competing

Hermit thrush and
red clover

samples. Other symbols also speak directly to the state's well-being: sugar maples, which yield syrup and incredible autumn scenery; Morgan horses, good-natured, hard-working, thrifty animals; milk, the linchpin of the economy. Vermont's coat of arms—designed by Charles Heyde, a Burlington landscape painter who married Walt Whitman's sister—depicts the view that probably greeted explorer Samuel de

Vermont coat of arms

"Freedom and Unity"

State motto

Marble replica of Leonardo da Vinci's *The Last Supper*, carved by Francesco Pinelli in 1956, is housed in Proctor, near the Rutland quarries. *Photo Jerry LeBlond. Below:* Sugar maple in autumn. *Photo Rob Badger*

Champlain as he took his first look at the future state: the outline of Mount Mansfield, the state's highest peak (4,083 feet), and Camel's Hump, the third-highest, rising boldly against a yellow sky. Flanking a pine tree are sheaves and a milk cow: emblems of all-important agriculture. The motto "Freedom and Unity" refers to Vermont's independence prior to joining the Union, and its perennial go-our-own-way spirit since becoming the 14th state. ❧

Sugar on Snow

Boil light maple syrup to 255° F.
Pour on top of pure snow.
Eat the sticky top layer.
Optional: Follow with a bite of sour pickle.

Red Flannel Hash

Traditionally this recipe was the thrifty way to recycle left-over corned beef from a New England boiled dinner. Since few corn their own beef these days, here is an adaptation from *The Fifty States Cookbook*. Homemade corned beef can certainly be used. Carrots are optional, beets essential.

6 medium beets, cooked
4 medium potatoes, cooked
1 cup cooked beef, diced
1 tsp. salt
¼ tsp. pepper
3 tbsp. butter or other fat
1 tbsp. cream

Chop vegetables, mix with diced beef, add seasonings. Melt 2 tbsp. butter in heavy skillet; add beef mixture; moisten slightly with hot water. Cover and cook slowly until meat is heated through and browned. Just before serving, add cream and 1 tbsp. butter; stir, heat, and serve.

Above: Brook Trout by **Stephen Huneck, 1998.** *Stephen Huneck Gallery, Woodstock. Right:* **The State Capitol in Montpelier.** *Photo Joe Sohm*

A Tale of Two Fish

Perhaps uniquely among the states, Vermont has two state fish: the "coldwater" Brook Trout and the "warmwater" Walleye Pike. Why? The state legislature gave no explanation other than calling both "handsome, sporty, and tasty" when making joint designation in 1978. The trout is indigenous and has been around since the glaciers. It's found in cold, clean streams throughout the state, averaging just under a pound. The pike, found naturally in Lake Champlain and stocked elsewhere (especially the Northeast Kingdom), generally weighs in at 4 to 8 pounds, with a record set at 12 pounds 8 ounces. Maybe Vermonters just love their fishing twice as much as other Americans.

A Minor Ode to the Morgan Horse

I may not incline
To the porcupine,
And I may be averse
To what is much worse:
The bear
That is rare,
The goat
That's remote,
The sheep, from which year after year
    you must remove the coat,
The catamount
That does not amount to that amount,
The cow
That somehow
We, as a human minority, cannot allow;
And although, as one of the
    Democratic minority
I should, alas,
Far prefer the jackass,
I must—until a state animal can choose
    its own state—
Not hesitate
To vote, of course,
For the Morgan horse.

William Jay Smith, 1960

"I LOVE VERMONT BECAUSE OF HER HILLS and valleys, her scenery and invigorating climate, but most of all because of her indomitable people....If the spirit of liberty should vanish in other parts of the union, and support of our institutions should languish, it could all be replenished from the generous store held by this brave little state of Vermont."

Native son (and 30th president) Calvin Coolidge, in an address from the Bennington train platform, 1928

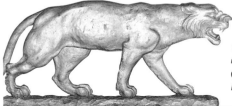

Above: Morgan colts. The founder of the breed, foaled in 1789, was named for his owner, schoolmaster Justin Morgan. His descendants are noted for their endurance—a thrifty breed for a thrifty state. *Photo F. B. Grunzweig. Left: Catamount.* Maker unknown, c. 1891. The catamount (cougar) is an unofficial but time-honored symbol. *Photo Erik Borg/Vermont Folklife Center*

c. 1300–1750 Iroquois- and Algonquian-speaking tribes settle in region.

1609 Samuel de Champlain explores the lake that now bears his name.

1666 The French establish first settlement, Fort St. Anne, on Isle la Motte.

1724 Massachusetts colonists establish first white settlement at Fort Dummer, near Brattleboro.

1737 Ethan Allen born.

1741 King George II assigns territory to New Hampshire.

1749 First New Hampshire Grant—23,040 acres around Bennington—awarded.

1752 First maple sugar made by a white settler, Samuel Robinson.

1763 Treaty of Paris; French relinquish Vermont claims.

1764–83 Vermont territory fought over by New Hampshire and New York.

1770 Estimated population 10,000.

1775 Ethan Allen and the Green Mountain Boys help capture Fort Ticonderoga from the British.

1776 Battle of Lake Champlain.

1777 Vermont residents declare their independence as a republic called New Connecticut. Battle of Bennington won by Americans.

1778 Thomas Chittenden elected first governor.

1780 State's first newspaper, the *Vermont Gazette,* appears briefly in Westminster. Estimated population 47,620.

1784–85 First bridge built across the Connecticut River, at Bellows Falls.

1785 First marble quarry in U.S. opens, in East Dorset.

1791 Vermont admitted to the Union as 14th state. Morgan horse patriarch brought to the state by Justin Morgan. First library opens in Brookfield. University of Vermont chartered.

1793 Bennington pottery makes its first appearance. Copper discovered in Strafford.

1794 The *Rutland Herald* begins publication as a weekly.

1800 Middlebury College founded. Population 154,465.

1808 Montpelier becomes the state capital.

1816 The year without a summer: crops fail, livestock perish, emigration accelerates.

1823 Champlain Canal opens.

1828 William Lloyd Garrison begins editing *Journal of the Times.*

1834 Blacksmith Thomas Davenport of Brandon invents first electric motor.

1840 Vermont Historical Society founded.

1850 Population 314,120.

1861 Civil War begins; Vermont is first state to offer troops to Lincoln.

1862 Vermont's senator Justin Morrill sponsors the Land Grant College Act.

1864 George Perkins Marsh publishes *Man and Nature.*

1872 Calvin Coolidge, 30th president, born in Plymouth.

1881 Chester A. Arthur born in Fairfield. Last known Vermont catamount shot, Barnard.

1890 Population 332,422. Seventy-five percent of Vermont land is cleared; deer have nearly vanished from state.

1910 Long Trail is begun; work continues until 1929.

1920 Bread Loaf School of English launches. Karl Martin begins manufacturing the "Wasp" automobile in Bennington.

1922 Vermont's first radio station, WCAX, broadcasts from Burlington.

1923 Calvin Coolidge sworn in as 30th president at Plymouth Notch.

1927 Great Flood causes widespread destruction in the state; leaves 9,000 homeless.

1932 Bennington College opens—women only, no grades.

1933 First ski tow in the U.S. opens at Woodstock. National Guard quells violent granite workers strike in Barre.

1946 *Vermont Life* magazine begins publication.

1947 Marlboro College founded.

1950 Population 377,747.

1954 Voters elect the first female lieutenant governor, Consuelo Northrop Bailey.

1964 Lyndon B. Johnson is first Democrat ever to receive a Vermont majority in a presidential election.

1970 State legislature passes a Land Use and Development Control Act for environmental protection. Population 444,330.

1977 Exiled Russian writer Alexander Solzhenitsyn moves to Cavendish.

1984 Madeleine Kunin is first woman elected governor.

1991 State celebrates its bicentennial. Population about 560,000.

Right: River otter *(Lutra canadensis)*, once a common denizen of the Champlain and Connecticut Rivers; settlement in the early 19th century greatly depleted its numbers. *Photo Michael Bisceglie. Below:* Daisies at Silver Lake, in the Green Mountain National Forest. *Photo George Wuerthner*

Vermont—from the French words for "green" and "mountain"—takes its name and much of its character from the lofty spine that bisects its slender length. Modest in land area, its geography is surprisingly varied. To the west, down rugged foothills that become rolling slopes and then arable lands, lies the relative vastness of New York State. Lake Champlain defines the north-

western border, giving Vermont indirect access to the Atlantic via a barge canal connecting to the Hudson River. East of the Green Mountains, past a series of north–south ridges, deep valleys, and fertile lowlands, is the Connecticut River, dividing Vermont from New Hampshire along the entire length of both states. Northward lies Quebec, giving Vermont the distinction of shouldering up to a foreign country—one of only 12 states to do so. To the south, choppy hills and winding back roads lead gently into neighboring Massachusetts. ❧

> *"If it is not the most beautiful state in the union, which is?"*
>
> *Bernard De Voto, 1954*

A View of Vermont by William Sonntag, 1874. Typical of its period, this landscape depicts Vermont as rugged wilderness; later painters would emphasize the state's pastoral side. *New Britain Museum of American Art*

"NEW HAMPSHIRE ONCE CLAIMED THAT HER INITIALS STOOD FOR Near Heaven and she thumbed her nose across the Connecticut and asked, 'How do you like that, old girl?'

"And Vermont complacently replied, 'Correct as hell, madam. You are right next to Vermont.'"

In A Vermont Encounter *by Horace Dunbar, 1938*

The Belated Party on Mansfield Mountain by Jerome B. Thompson, 1858. Like many of his artistic peers, Thompson took aesthetic liberties with the mountain, making it conform to the period's expectations of wildness. *The Metropolitan Museum of Art, New York*

Unto the Hills

When they arose more than 300 million years ago, the Green Mountains—the upper reaches of the Appalachians—were nearly as tall as the Swiss Alps. Worn down by a great glacier that advanced across the land during the Pleistocene, the jagged peaks emerged rounded, shorter, with deep gashes in the rock made by floods of melting ice. At the same time, the valleys were deepened by the weight of the water, which submerged the land and surrounded the mountaintops, stranding them like islands. This terrain proved ideal for growing forests: conifers at higher elevations and deciduous hardwoods lower down. Today the Green Mountains rank with other weathered ranges of the East for height—the tallest

peak, Mount Mansfield, reaches 4,393 feet—and offer great challenges to outdoor adventurers. The Long Trail traverses the major peaks for 260 miles, from Massachusetts to the Canadian line. Created in the early 1900s by a woodsman who wanted a ready-made pathway through the thickest forests, the Long Trail later inspired the Appalachian Trail, with which it is concurrent for 146 miles. From the trail, breaks in the ridges offer splendid views of the Adirondacks, across the New York border.

"HERE IN VERMONT, OUR CULTURE AND OUR ACCENTS are different on either side of the Green Mountains. Even our language—our words and usage   are different here in St. Johnsbury from, say, over in Burlington. On this side, we are geared toward Boston and always have been....Whereas on the other side of Vermont, it's Albany and New York City."

Graham Newell, Latin teacher and state senator,
born 1915, St. Johnsbury, in Vermonters: Oral Histories
from Down Country to Northeast Kingdom, *1986*

Above: **Hiker on the Long Trail, near Killington Peak.** *Photo Jerry LeBlond. Right:* **Bluebells and hairgrass, Green Mountains.** *Photo Tim Seaver*

Village of Stowe, Vermont by Luigi Lucioni, 1931. Lucioni was one of many painters who summered in Vermont in the 1920s and 30s and later took up permanent residence. *The Minneapolis Institute of Arts*

Vermont's lowland landscape is a billowing counterpane of rolling hills, emerald fields, ribbonlike roads, farm buildings, fences, and wildflowers. The family farm may have yielded to the business farm, but agriculture—chiefly dairying—remains close to Vermont's soul. Not that farming has ever been easy here. The subsoil is rocky, and outcroppings make machine tilling problematic; barely half the state's land is cultivable. Yet

Vermonters have made good use of the glacier's legacy in the stone walls that mark property lines and draw undulating patterns over the hills. Stone walls have also inspired poets, as in Robert Frost's ruminating on what they keep in, what they keep out. Public policy has banned roadside advertising and enacted other measures to sustain the state's rural character. ❧

Stone walls are as much a part of the Vermont landscape as hedgerows are in rural England. They make good use of the native stone, which had to be painstakingly cleared to allow cultivation. This stone wall separates a Halifax farm building from its neighbors. *Photo Paul R. Turnball*

I farm a pasture where the boulders lie
As touching as a basketful of eggs...

Robert Frost, from "Of the Stones of the Place," 1942

"BUT IS VERMONT STONY? There are many thousands of acres, in Vermont, without stone enough to build a wall around them. As the hill farms go there is almost always enough land free from stones to make a well balanced farm. The stony part left to pasture and forest is all the better for its stones."

Wallace Nutting,
Vermont Beautiful, 1922

> *"I like Vermont because the trees are close together and the people are far apart."*
>
> Vermont schoolgirl

Man in the Woods by Thomas Waterman Wood, c. 1855. By the mid-19th century, when this painting was made, Vermont's forests were already second-growth. *Wood Gallery and Arts Center, Montpelier*

The Woodland Kingdom

Vermont's primeval forests were mostly cleared during early settlement. A few ancient stands endure in the Northeast Kingdom, the densely vegetated area that borders Canada, but later growth predominates. No matter what their age, the trees turn spectacular colors every autumn, usually around the first week in October. The annual miracle draws thousands

of "leaf-peepers"—the indigenous term—who goggle at the incandescent maples and birches. Vermont's classic village backdrops provide the perfect accent to nature's drama. One picturesque view in Peacham is called Kodak Corner locally because of its frequent appearance on calendar pages.

Across the state wildlife is thriving, as lands once given over to farming revert to forest. Moose have reappeared, especially in the wild northeast. Ravens, osprey, and falcons have established new ranges. Rivers and streams are again full of fish. Coyotes roam everywhere and black bears are fairly common. There are even reported sightings of catamounts (actually cougars), the legendary cat that figured large in Ethan Allen's time and has haunted the Vermont imagination since.

"ALL THE HILLS BLUSH; I THINK THAT autumn must be the best season to journey over even the Green Mountains. You frequently exclaim to yourself, 'What red maples!'"

Henry David Thoreau

Left: Barred owl, well camouflaged within a dense Vermont forest. *Photo Ted Levin. Below:* Lye Brook Falls cuts a foamy ribbon in the Lye Brook Wilderness, part of the Green Mountain National Forest. *Photo George Wuerthner*

Perfect hunting weather: a boy and his dog set out into a frozen landscape. *Camel's Hump* by Rowland E. Robinson, c. 1875. Robinson wrote and illustrated stories about 19th-century Vermont. His farmhouse in Rokeby is now a museum. *Rowland E. Robinson Memorial Association, Rokeby*

Depending on how you look at it, the Vermont year has "six months of winter and six months of getting ready for winter," or "nine months of winter and three months of poor sledding." Count on it that the weather is chilly much of the time, the ground often covered by snow. In 1996 the lowest recorded temperature was 35 degrees below zero. The higher the elevation, the chillier it gets, and the Green Mountains cast a rain shadow that makes precipitation lighter in the western lee. Throughout the state the growing season is short—even shorter in the far north—but it is congenial to certain crops (apples, lettuce, maple syrup) and cool-weather pursuits. Snowy winters make for postcard views and a recreational paradise, while Vermont's nonwinter seasons are less romanticized but equally extravagant: spring a muddy burst of warmth (known universally as "Mud Season"), summer leafy green and warm, autumn a spectacular array of reds, oranges, and yellows set against a sky of crystalline blue. ❧

"[THE COLORS] ARE LIKE KINGDOM FAIR. THEY COME ONCE A YEAR FOR LESS than a week; then they're gone. And even while they're here they aren't quite real. You can't paint them. I've tried, and they always come out like a picture postcard. It's when they go that's the best time to paint this country. After the rain and wind have torn down the leaves and left the hills and farm bare. Then maybe you can paint it like it is...."

Howard Frank Mosher, Where the Rivers Flow North, *1978*

Above: A Vermont twilight. *Photo Peter Miller/Panoramic images. Right:* W. A. Bentley (1865–1931), nicknamed the Snowflake King, made 5,300 micro-photographic studies of snowflakes and became an authority on the subject. He would catch the delicate snowflakes on a cold board covered with black velvet, and photograph them in a refriger-ated camera room. This speci-men was photographed in 1890. *Buffalo Museum of Science*

Beaded Abenaki head-
band, artist unknown,
c. 1900. Crafted of
worsted twill, the
shaped headband is
bound with purple vel-
vet and trimmed with
beads. Its design signi-
fied the power of the
plant world. *Museum
of Civilization, National
Museums of Canada
Below:* Abenaki snow-
shoes, c. 1925. *Erik Borg/
Vermont Folklife Center*

The First Vermonters

Ancestral Vermont once was thought to be a place
bereft of indigenous people—a "land in between"—but
archaeologists have turned up sure signs of early native
activity. The most ancient traces suggest that an Eskimo
culture inhabited much of New England before moving
north into Canada. Around 2000 B.C., a pre-Algonquian
group left ceremonial whale-tail artifacts and fishing
lures in various parts of the state. More recent evidence of
a once-vital Indian culture includes village sites, fighting
and hunting tools, and burial remains unearthed
along lakesides and riverbanks. Still, it's believed
that the Abenaki, Algonquian, and Iroquois knew
Vermont chiefly as a route rather than a residence—a place to hunt, fish, and pass through on
their way elsewhere. Well into the 18th century,
the land was still unclaimed wilderness. In the
great ensuing struggle for this part of the New
World, the Abenaki aligned themselves with the
French, their Algonquian foes with the British. ❧

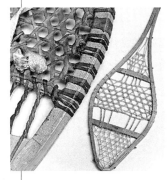

Abenaki natives tapping maple trees and planting crops, 1724, from a French work, *Moeurs des Sauvages Ameriquains. Special Collections, Bailey/Howe Library, University of Vermont Museum. Below:* Quilled birch-bark box, artist unknown, 19th century. Decorated with quills and embroidery, these Eastern Woodland Algonquian boxes became popular trade items. *Hood Museum of Art, Dartmouth College*

"I WOULD TRAVEL DOWN A DIFFERENT PATH IF I didn't have to make what people will buy. People don't understand if I make something from my heritage. They understand pipes, Western-beadwork....That's 'Indian' to them."

John Lawyer, contemporary artisan of Abenaki and Mohawk descent, in Always in Season: Folk Art and Traditional Culture in Vermont, *1982*

French and English, Yorkers and Grants

The first white man in Vermont was the French explorer Samuel de Champlain, who in 1609 sailed into the lake that now bears his name. The Vermont territory lay strategically between two important water routes—the lake and the Connecticut River—a fact recognized early. The French built forts along key waterways against Indian raids, but were driven out by the British in 1763. Once in control, the British started parceling out land, but ownership in the "New Hampshire Grants" became mired in confusion, with royals across the ocean making vague and contradictory grants to too many colonists. George II gave the land due west to New Hampshire in 1741, while George III granted the land "due east" to New York in 1764, but neither king specified east or west of what. With both Yorkers and Grants laying claim to the same stony parcels and issuing grants to speculators, fierce skirmishes among settlers became common.

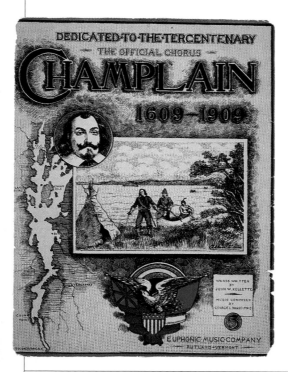

A South View of the New Fortress at Crown Point, with the Camp, Commanded by Major General Amherst in the Year 1759. Drawn on the spot by Thos. Davies, Capt. Lieut. of the Royal Artillery

Song of the Vermonters

Ho—all to the borders! Vermonters come down,
With your breeches of deerskin and jackets of brown:
With your red woolen cap and your moccasins, come,
To the gathering summons of trumpet and drum....

Come York or come Hampshire, come traitors or knaves,
If ye ruled o'er our land, ye shall rule o'er our graves;
Our vow is recorded—our banner unfurled,
In the name of Vermont we defy all the world!

"Song of the Vermonters," 1779

South view of the fortress and camp at Crown Point, watercolor by Thomas Davies, 1759. Winterthur Museum

"The gods of the hills are not the gods of the valleys."

Ethan Allen

In 1770, a band of homesteaders, confident of their claim to this land "in between," arose to fend off the Yorkers. Ethan Allen and his Green Mountain Boys harrassed the New York grant-holders, chasing them back across the borders. But before the land dispute was resolved, the first salvo of the American Revolution broke out, and the Vermonters turned their attention to the bigger fight. In 1775 Allen and his men, aided by Benedict Arnold, took Fort Ticonderoga from the British. Ethan Allen has since passed into legend. Described as daring, ardent, and unyielding, the "voice of Vermont," he was said to be able to wrestle panthers and chew nails. In truth, he was a land speculator and a renegade—but above all a fighter with an unquenchable love of freedom. ❦

Above: Ethan Allen's men hoisted a prominent New Yorker in a chair and left him to dangle for several hours, c. 1840. The catamount on the sign was the Vermonters' emblem. *University of Vermont, Special Collections. Right: Statue of Ethan Allen by Larkin G. Mead, c. 1876. Once standing triumphant atop the capitol in Montpelier, it now resides in Statuary Hall at the U.S. Capitol. National Statuary Hall Collection*

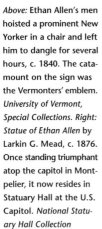

"FRIENDS AND FELLOW SOLDIERS, YOU HAVE...BEEN A scourge and terror to arbitrary power. Your valour has been famed abroad, and acknowledged...by the advice and orders to me to surprise and take the garrison now before us. I now propose to advance before you, and in person conduct you through the wicket-gate; for we must this morning either quit our pretensions to valour, or possess ourselves of this fortress in a few minutes....You that will undertake voluntarily, poise your firelocks."

Ethan Allen to his men, before the capture of Fort Ticonderoga, 1775

Above: Ethan Allen and the Green Mountain Boys Capturing Fort Ticonderoga, by Frederick Coffay Yohn, c. early 1900s. In 1925, the Ticonderoga Pencil Company commissioned this poster. *Left: Ruins of Fort Ticonderoga,* by Thomas H. Burridge, 1864. *Both, Vermont Historical Society*

Battle of Bennington by Alonzo Chappel, 1854. The 1777 battle was a turning point in the Revolutionary War. *Bennington Museum* **Right: Copper coin minted by the independent nation of "New Connecticut" (Vermont) 1781–88.** *Vermont Historical Society*

A State in the End

Vermont's role in the Revolutionary War was ambivalent, as England tried to convince Vermonters that their claim to statehood would be refused by the Continental Congress. Despite Ethan Allen's early efforts, he and the Grants saw little action for much of the war. Vermont's key moment was the Battle of Bennington, where Colonel John Stark's troops routed the British under Burgoyne. It broke the British forces' momentum in their advance down the

Champlain Valley, deprived them of provisions and ammunition, thwarted their aim of cutting off New England from the other colonies, and pierced their morale. Due to its disputed status, Vermont was denied a place among the signers of the Declaration of Independence in 1776. So the following year Vermont declared its own independence from England as a separate nation called "New Connecticut"—later Vermont. The land claims were resolved in 1790; a year later Vermont became the fourteenth state. Its waterways and shipbuilding aided the young nation in its next run-in with England, the War of 1812, but Vermont beef was also smuggled north across the border to feed the enemy.

Captain Elijah Dewey **by Ralph Earl, 1798. Dewey, son of Bennington's first minister, was a captain in the Bennington militia at the battles of Bennington, Ticonderoga, and Saratoga. In peacetime he was the proprietor of Dewey's Tavern (now the Walloomsac Inn) in Old Bennington, shown in the background.** *Bennington Museum.* **Below: Bennington Monument.** *Photo Margo Taussig Pinkerton*

> "I AM AS DETERMINED TO PRESERVE THE Independence of Vermont as Congress is that of the Union and rather than fail I will retire with my hardy green mountain boys into the caverns of the mountains and make war on all mankind."
>
> *Ethan Allen, in a 1781 letter to the Continental Congress, referring to rumors that New York and New Hampshire might split Vermont between them*

Growing the State

Vermont's constitution, adopted in 1777, reflected a passion for justice based on its own struggles. It was the first state in America to abolish slavery, establish universal voting rights (for males), and authorize public schools. Strong moral beliefs surfaced early: Vermont was strongly abolitionist by the late 1830s and banned liquor in 1852. The population grew quickly after statehood, jumping nearly threefold in the next two decades. This vibrant growth soon slowed, then virtually stopped following the Great Famine of 1816—"the year without a summer." Many who had come to farm moved on to more fertile lands in the Midwest. The resourceful who stayed on

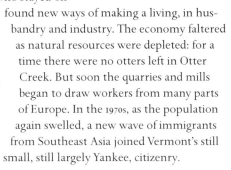

found new ways of making a living, in husbandry and industry. The economy faltered as natural resources were depleted: for a time there were no otters left in Otter Creek. But soon the quarries and mills began to draw workers from many parts of Europe. In the 1970s, as the population again swelled, a new wave of immigrants from Southeast Asia joined Vermont's still small, still largely Yankee, citizenry.

"PUT THE VERMONTERS IN FRONT AND keep the ranks closed up."

Civil War slogan passed down in Vermont

Above: Haymakers—Mount Mansfield, Vermont by Jerome B. Thompson, 1859. *Private collection.* This optimistic vision of Vermont farm life proved cruelly false to many settlers, great numbers of whom relocated to the Midwest for a fresh start. *Right: Vermont Lawyer* by Horace Bundy, 1841. *National Gallery of Art, Washington, D.C. Opposite:* Vermont enlisted man in the Union Army, and his wife. *Herb Peck Collection*

Below: Indian Summer by Frank E. Larson, 1993. Water, open fields, dark woods, farm buildings, and distant hills compose a quintessential Vermont landscape. Courtesy the artist Opposite above: Logging Camp in Vermont by Henry Hitchings, 1867. The Merchants Bank, Burlington. Opposite below: Handmade farm implements like this wooden spade plow, made between 1780 and 1820, demonstrate the inventiveness and superb craftsmanship of Vermont settlers. *Shelburne Museum*

Vermont's early settlers grew and processed their own food, made their own clothing, and raised small cash crops to pay for things they could not produce themselves. Later they got down to the business of generating money from the state's ample resources: thick forests, rushing rivers, and workable soil. As early as 1778 the Winooski River and its lower falls were harnessed for lumber milling and woodworking. In the early 1800s agriculture took hold in both the upland hills and the fertile valleys of the Connecticut River and the Champlain basin. Major crops included apples, potatoes, and maple

syrup. During this time most of Vermont's first-growth forests were felled to burn for potash, and when sodium replaced potash in the making of soap and glass, for lumber. The trees—mostly hardwoods including maple, beech, and birch—grew back, to be harvested again for lumber or cleared for building.

In part because of this early plunder, Vermonters are vigilant about their woodlands. In the 1960s, the state legislature, acting for a population inclined toward country ways, passed measures to slow development, control clearcutting, and provide incentives for prudent land use. ❧

Maple Sugaring

Legend has it that "sugaring off" began when an Indian hurled his tomahawk at a maple, causing sap from the gash to flow into a cooking vessel left under the tree. His wife, thinking the liquid was water, put some venison in the pot to cook, and the sweet sap, boiling down to syrup, imparted a new and beguiling flavor to the meat. Exactly how the leap was made to more organized means of sugaring we don't know. Sugaring, said one writer, is "one part money-maker and one

part open-air ritual for the soul." Sap flows freely in maples beginning the first thawing days of March. Temperature swings move the sap up from the roots into the trunk and eventually through the entire tree; ideal conditions are warm, sunny days with freezing nights. Sugar makers bore holes in the trees, drive spouts, and hang sap buckets from them—or, in the modern manner, insert plastic tubing into the holes and let the sap run into collecting tanks. Sap is then boiled down and filtered for syrup or maple sugar products.

Left: Maple syrup can. *New England Container Co. Below:* Syrup arranged by grade. *Photo Orah Moore Opposite above: Sugar House by Aldro T. Hibbard, 1950. Southern Vermont Art Center. Opposite below:* Maple sugaring scene (detail), artist unknown, c. 1910. Crafted in wood, the scene includes a tiny scale, a nosy squirrel, and sap buckets hung from a small forest of maples. *Shelburne Museum*

"YOU CAN TELL WHEN THE WEATHER FEELS like sugar weather. It's the air. It's an urge that tells you you'd better be getting up there. I don't know. There's something about it that just puts that feeling right into you. 'Well, we'd better be getting up to the sugar place and start in.'"

Everett Palmer, sugar maker from Waitsfield, born 1907

Grading Vermont's Syrup

Vermont's Department of Agriculture, Food, and Markets distinguishes four grades of maple syrup:

Fancy. U.S. Grade A Light Amber: Light amber color, delicate bouquet. For use on foods that won't overwhelm its subtle flavor.

Grade A Medium Amber: Medium amber color, pronounced maple bouquet, characteristic maple flavor. For table and all-around use.

Grade B Dark Amber: Dark amber color, robust bouquet, hearty flavor. For table and all-around use.

Grade B: Strong and dark. For cooking or adding maple flavor to processed foods.

Wealth on the Hoof

Vermont has not always been as identified with dairy cows as it is today, though animal husbandry in some form has long figured in its economy. Beef cows came first. When other states gained an edge in the beef market, Merino sheep were imported and raised in huge numbers. When sheep breeding went bust, Vermonters turned to dairying, producing milk, cheese, and butter for all of New England. Milk production more than quadrupled from 1950 to 1980, when cows came to symbolize the very idea of the state. Less numerous but also emblematic of Vermont is the Morgan horse. Named for the itinerant schoolmaster who owned the founding sire 200 years ago, the breed is noted for its strength, intelligence, gentleness, and ability to pass on these qualities to its offspring. One Vermonter who raises Morgans calls them "thrifty" animals

"who eat next to nothing and stay fat."
Well matched to the local geography,
these smart, willing animals helped
many farmers make a go of their mar-
ginal land: hauling logs and plowing
rocky fields.

"A MORGAN HORSE CAN SKID ANYTHING
these woods can grow. Morgans love to
pull. You can see it in their eyes. They
pull for the sake of pulling, to please
themselves."

Howard Frank Mosher,
Where the Rivers Flow North, *1978*

Above: **The Morgan story
is told by Vermonter
Marguerite Henry in her
well-known book for
children,** *Justin Morgan
Had a Horse.* **Illustration
by Wesley Dennis, 1954.**
Left: Grazing **by Woody
Jackson, 1988. Jackson's
flatly rendered black-
and-white bovines are
familiar to fans of Ben
and Jerry's Homemade
ice cream, a fixture
throughout Vermont.**
Holy Cow, Inc.

A Marble Quarry by James Hope, 1851. The block of stone being lifted here from Sheldon and Slason's quarry in West Rutland was destined for the Washington Monument. *Museum of Fine Arts, Boston*

Stone-quarrying—mostly marble and granite, but also slate, talc, and asbestos—became an important industry in the late 19th century, bringing European immigrants to work the earth, along with their exotic influences in food, music, religion, language. Quarrying was centered around Rutland and Barre, where Scottish stoneworkers erected a granite statue to a fellow Scot, the poet Robert

Burns. In Sharon stands a huge monument to Vermont-born Joseph Smith, the founder of Mormonism. Entire towns, such as Proctor, West Rutland, and Middlebury, were once showcases for local stonecraft. Vermont stone is also found in major buildings around the country, including New York's Public Library and the United Nations buildings. Local artists have long been inspired by their native stone: Brattleboro sculptor Larkin Mead gained fame by creating a snow angel in Vermont marble, and Hiram Powers used the same to render his *Greek Slave,* eight times. ❦

Massive Ionic columns of Vermont marble front the Electra Havemeyer Webb Memorial, an outstanding Greek Revival building in Shelburne. *Shelburne Museum Photo Ken Burris. Left: Braintree Panthers* by Jim Sardonis, 1991. The sculptor, a Randolph resident, himself quarried the Braintree pink granite for this family of cougars. *Courtesy the artist*

Blacksmith's Boy—Heel and Toe by Norman Rockwell, 1940. Rockwell posed this scene of a competition between blacksmiths at Moon's shop in South Shaftsbury and used his neighbors as models. The same fellow, Harvey McKee, waves dollar bills in foreground and, de-mustached, smokes a cigarette at right. The artist himself appears at left, in the dark-banded hat. *Norman Rockwell Trust*

Yankee Ingenuity

While many left Vermont in the great westward migration of the early 1800s, some of those who stayed showed a knack for invention. The first patent ever taken out in the U.S. Patent Office went to a Vermonter for a process to make more and better potash. Diverse small-scale industries took root in river towns like Brattleboro—known for producing organ pipes among other items—and Bellows Falls. Weighing scales were devised and manufactured in St. Johnsbury and Rutland. Other important manufactured goods were machine tools, firearms, and furniture. Windsor especially was a center of invention, producing the hydraulic pump, coffee percolator, glazier's point and driver, as well as machinery to make cars, airplanes, and other mass-produced items. The town was also the cradle of the firearms industry; the Kendall sporting rifle and the long-range Sharps rifle were made here. Recently

Vermont has had its own small high-tech boom, with companies turning out computer hardware clustered around the village of Essex Junction. Throughout the state, craftspeople spin, weave, carve, throw pots, and package locally prepared food to feed a growing taste for handmade products. Rustic or refined, things "Made in Vermont" are in demand.

"MONTPELIER CRACKERS
ESTABLISHED 1828
CROSS BAKING CO.
BEST IN THE WORLD"

Sign on a Montpelier bakery

Above: Trade Sign, Bicycle Livery, Carriage and Paint Shop. Maker unknown, c. 1895–1905. *Museum of American Folk Art, New York. Left: Chapel Organ* built by Jacob Estey Organ Company of Brattleboro, 1884. Estey turned out organs with masterfully carved cabinetry housing the latest reed organ technology. *Old Stone House Museum. Photo Erik Borg*

The first tourists to invade the Green Mountain State were lured by the mineral springs around Brattleboro. The advent of the railroad in 1848 brought visitors to newly built resorts in Manchester, Woodstock, and Stowe to enjoy the scenery and mountain air. In the days before car travel, local inns would advertise carriage service from the "depot," fresh butter from Vermont cows, and, beginning in 1933, ski lifts for those who wished to try the new sport. Since the first "flatlanders" set foot in the state, Vermonters have felt ambivalent about them. Some applauded the social life that

Above: Signpost at the Dorset Inn, founded in 1796, depicts an early innkeeper. *Photo Lee Snider/Imageworks. Right:* Fall color on a country road near Groton. *Photo Ric Ergenbright. Opposite:* "Nose-Dive Annie"—Mrs. J. Negley Cooke of Cleveland at Stowe, Vermont by Louise Dahl-Wolfe, 1941. Dahl-Wolfe's spread on ski fashions in a 1941 *Harper's Bazaar* launched the boom in stylish skiwear. *Center for Creative Photography, University of Arizona*

summer people imported, and their lively interest in cultural pursuits. Others saw dollar signs: Vermont was the first state to establish an official publicity service to encourage tourism. But a strain of xenophobia persists in various forms: ignoring or poking gentle fun at outsiders. ❧

"FOR VERMONTERS THE PUT-ON HAS BECOME A FOLK-ART, PARTICULARLY when victims of it are outlanders....[T]he most famous Vermont hoax [from 1887] is a tale about human hibernation. It tells how Vermonters would freeze their oldsters for the winter and thaw them out in the spring in time to help with the planting of crops. The tale still circulates in the guise of truth, and outlanders ask incredulously if it is true."

Charles T. Morrissey, Vermont: A Bicentennial History, *1981*

A tall-spired white clapboard church, usually Congregational, is a landmark in most Vermont towns, a legacy of early settlers. But Vermont's overwhelmingly Protestant look is deceptive. In fact, the first church services in the territory were Roman Catholic masses, held in 1666 at Fort Saint Anne, and a majority of Vermonters today worship as Catholics. Churches play a traditional role in small-town life, helping in times of need, sponsoring covered-dish suppers, and organizing rummage sales. Native faiths also arose here. Mormon patriarchs Joseph Smith and Brigham Young were born in Vermont. The end-of-the-

One of the state's prized architectural specimens, the Old Round Church, in Richmond, was a joint undertaking in 1813 by five Protestant denominations that worshipped together until one by one each broke away, abandoning the extraordinary 16-sided building. Renovated in 1981, it is now a meeting house. *Photo George A. Robinson/f/stop Pictures, Inc. Right: Easter Dawn Mass: St. Francis de Sales Church* by Leroy Williams, 1852. *Bennington Museum*

world Millerites flourished under Calais-based William Miller. John Humphrey Noyes's Perfectionist movement got its start in Putney, but its members fled en masse to more hospitable pastures in New York. ✤

"NOTHING COULD DIFFER MORE FROM THE VERMONT TRADITION than the intensity of Mormon belief in the doctrine of a single church, unquestioned, even undiscussed…submitted to in enthusiastic docility by all the community."

Dorothy Canfield Fisher, Vermont Tradition, *1953*

Church Supper by Paul Sample, 1933. Sample summered near Westmore, which here hosts a church supper for locals and elegant summer folk. Like his contemporaries Norman Rockwell, Luigi Lucioni, and Andrew Wyeth, Sample painted rural New England in a regionalist style. *Museum of Fine Arts, Springfield*

Our Town at Dawn by Cleland Selby, 1981. This six-foot-long hooked rug illustrates the maker's concept of a Vermont village, with school, church, mill, sugar house, cemetery, covered bridge, and houses. Selby is the third generation in his family to hook rugs.
Photo Erik Borg/Vermont Folklife Center

The Village Green

Vermont has 241 towns, 8 cities, and a handful of "gores"— odd-shaped, unique-to-Vermont parcels of land that fall between town boundaries. Early settlers, craving homesteads but not necessarily neighbors, fanned out from a central point when choosing places to build or farm. In the southern part of the state, influenced by Connecticut and Massachusetts, town centers were planned around a fenced-off meeting or grazing ground, with churches, courthouse, town hall, library, school, and general store surrounding it. Farther north, village greens evolved more organically—usually at a point where roads met—and are thus less symmetrical. While the larger cities, notably Burlington, have grown significantly in recent years, most Vermont towns remain small; 68 percent of the current 589,000 Vermonters live in communities of fewer than 2,500 people.

On Woodstock green
the summer's past,

Even there it could not last,
Even there the leaves must lie
Prone beneath an autumn sky.
And through the park the scuffing feet
Of children find the dead leaves sweet,
As once I found them, on my way
With playmates of another day...

Ann Batchelder, "East of Bridgewater," c. 1940s

Above: **Craftsbury Common.** *Photo Alan Graham.* **Left: The Village Post Office** by Thomas Waterman Wood, 1873. Wood, the son of a Montpelier cabinet-maker, rose to prominence in the art world and was head of the National Academy. Portraiture was his bread-and-butter, but his enduring reputation hangs on his skillful genre scenes of Vermont life. *New York State Historical Association*

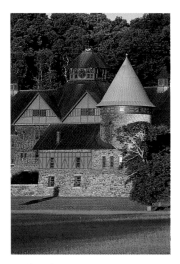

A network of winding roads and picturesque bridges stitches together Vermont's towns and villages. Travel in Vermont is a unique reminder of what New England was like before roadside advertising and commercial clutter ruled the landscape. Great efforts are taken to protect the state's 114 covered bridges—more than in any other state and many still used to span rivers such as the Lemon Fair, the Lamoille, and the Green. Often built as railroad crossings, these bridges have had their rails removed and are now used only by cars. (The last federal rail routes in Vermont were discontinued in 1971.) The nation's longest covered bridge crosses the Connecticut River at Windsor; it was built in 1866, at the peak of covered bridge design, with a 460-foot span. ❧

Scenic Drives

At the risk of slighting many, here are a few:

Route 108 through Smugglers' Notch, between Stowe and Jeffersonville

Route 100 through Granville Gulf

Route 121 through Saxtons River and Grafton

Route 2, island-hopping through the Grand Isles of Lake Champlain

I-89 between White River Junction and St. Albans (for fall foliage)

The Peacham Road, between Danville and Groton

Route 118 through Montgomery: views of six covered bridges

Green Bridge by Sabra Field, 1998. Field is a South Royalton printmaker whose Vermont scenes are widely collected. In 1998 two of her works traveled into space on the shuttle *Columbia. Opposite above:* The lavishly gabled and turreted Farm Barn at Shelburne Farms is among the nation's grandest barns. *Photo Gail Mooney. Opposite below:* The Cornish–Windsor covered bridge. *Photo Joe Sohm/Panoramic Images*

It was once Vermont's custom, they say, to choose senators and governors alternately from the west and east sides of the Green Mountains, to keep everyone happy. Wherever they hailed from, they were almost always Republicans, though Vermont politics have been an odd blend of fiscal conservatism and social liberalism. Its leaders, including marble magnate Redfield Proctor, internationalist Warren Austin, land-grant-college sponsor Justin Morrill, and horticulturist George D. Aiken, all ran as Republicans while endorsing such progressive causes as the abolition of slavery, educational opportunity, and environmental protection. Not until 1974 did a Democrat, Patrick Leahy, represent Vermont in the Senate. (He still does.) Madeleine Kunin, elected governor in 1985, was the first woman in that office, a nonnative (always noteworthy here), and a Democrat. Vermont has produced two U.S. presidents: the wildly popular Calvin Coolidge and Chester Arthur, who succeeded James Garfield, a former Vermont schoolteacher. ❧

Town Meeting

A classic expression of participatory democracy, town meeting is a treasured Vermont tradition. Once a year, on the first Tuesday after the first Monday in March, offices, banks, and schools shut down for Town Meeting Day, a state holiday. Selectmen from each town present what is called the "warning," an agenda that includes mostly local and state issues but also matters of national concern.

"WHEN I FIRST WENT TO WORK FOR HIM, I DIDN'T LIKE him because if I went in to tell him something and he was reading a paper, he would just go on reading. That annoyed the hell out of me. I discovered later he'd heard every word I said. It's a typical Vermont trait. They never let you know they're paying close attention to you. And yet they hear every word you say."

Lola Aiken on her husband, Senator George Aiken

Above: Calvin Coolidge by Dwight Case Sturges, 1925. *National Portrait Gallery Left:* Frame from "Doonesbury," July 5, 1981. Garry Trudeau's famous strip first appeared in the *Burlington Free Press;* this cartoon, on the election of Bernie Sanders as Burlington's first socialist mayor, pokes gentle fun at the candidate, the town, and talk-show host Tom Snyder. *© 1981 G. B. Trudeau. By permission of Universal Press Syndicate. Opposite:* The 1779 meeting house in Strafford. *Photo Lee Snider*

Upscale farmhouse renovations are taking place all over Vermont. *Right:* Interior of Twin Farms in Barnard, 1986, by architect Alan Wanzenberg. *Photo Pieter Estersohn Below: Blanket Chest with Drawers,* attributed to Thomas Matteson of South Shaftsbury, c. 1825. Cabinetmakers often painted their simple pine furniture with designs or to resemble the grain of more exotic woods. *Museum of American Folk Art, New York*

At Home in the Country

Farmhouse architecture grew up naturally to conform with its surroundings, hill after rolling hill. By the late 1700s, Vermont rural houses were spacious one-and-a-half or two-story buildings fashioned from beech or pine milled into planks, in the plain or gable-front box style of early New England dwellings. Most were painted white and lacked the more sophisticated detailing of dwellings farther south. Inside, they featured rough pine floorboards, crude fireplaces, and handwrought iron hinges. For a time in the early 1800s, house, barn, and shed were often linked together to form one long, sheltering space that kept families warm and dry as they went about their work, but such "continuous architecture" was eventually abandoned as unsanitary. The isolation of farm life was eased by the Order of the Patrons of Husbandry, better known as the Grange, which for generations guided business, politics, and social life. All-you-can-eat Grange suppers still draw people out in the remote Northeast Kingdom. A similar communal spirit

fueled the back-to-the-land movement of the 1960s and 70s, which attracted hippies from many states to the Vermont countryside. Their patron saints were Vermonters Helen and Scott Nearing, whose *Living the Good Life* became a homesteading bible.

> "WE HAD BUILT UP OUR GOOD LIFE IN VERMONT, IMPROVING THE SOIL, clearing out and enlarging the sugar orchard, replacing wooden shacks…and generally converting a sickly, bankrupt farm into a vigorous, healthy enterprise that was paying its own way and more."
>
> *Helen and Scott Nearing,* Living the Good Life, *1970*

Above: Tulips and old garden bench in a private garden. *Photo Alan Graham. Left:* Round barn built in 1901 by Fred "Silo" Quimby in East Passumpsic. Round barns were popular in the late 19th and early 20th centuries for permitting economy of labor; the first were built by Shakers. This barn was relocated from Passumpsic to Shelburne in the 1980s; it's now part of the Shelburne Museum. *Photo Ken Burris*

An 1826 Federal style home in Middlebury. *Photo John Dominis Below: Norman Rockwell Visits a Family Doctor by Norman Rockwell, 1947. Curtis Publishing Co./ Norman Rockwell Family Trust*

At Home in Town

Prosperous citizens of the 19th century gave towns such as Bennington, Manchester, Stowe, and Woodstock impressive village greens ringed with Federal style homes. Castleton is a showcase for the work of Thomas Reynold Dake, a Vermonter who made free use of classic architectural formulas. Vermonters had little interest in ornamentation, instead taking from established styles the overall forms and a sense of general proportion and good taste. Industrial cities such as Brattleboro and Rutland are a mix of red brick, white clapboard, and native marble or granite. The impulse toward historic preservation is strong in the state, and old buildings are often adapted to new uses rather than torn down.

Manchester's hilltop green is dominated by the stately Equinox Hotel, created in the late 1800s by Samuel Orvis. His son George's fly-fishing enterprise gained worldwide fame. *Photo Mark McCarty. Below: Musical Tall Case Clock by Nichols Goddard, c. 1808. Bennington Museum*

"I SEE NO TRUTH AT ALL TO THE MYTH THAT NEW Englanders are taciturn—they love gossip as well as anyone I ever knew—but the talk takes place mostly on neutral ground: in stores and barnyards, at auctions and church suppers. Your house is private. Vermonters are less likely to drop in unannounced for coffee than most other Americans, or to have you over for the evening. There are about two hundred people in Thetford Center, and I would guess I know a hundred and ninety of them. But I have not been in more than a dozen houses, and most people have never been in mine."

Noel Perrin, Amateur Sugar Maker, *1972*

Right: Mariner's oil lamp in pewter by contemporary craftsman Fred Danforth. Danforth is descended from an 18th-century New England pewtersmith. *Danforth Pewterers Below: Four-pat Butter Mold* by John Varnum, c. 1929. The Peacham area has long been known for its butter prints. Varnum, one of the finest carvers, sold his mold designs to customers as far off as California. *Peacham Historical Society*

Before such objects as baskets, wood furniture, hooked rugs, or needlework were considered "crafts" or "collectibles," they served as pragmatic responses to routine domestic hardship. Inadequate heating made bed coverings, coverlets, and handwoven blankets essentials in every Vermont home. The expense of imported goods required that bare floors be covered with woven or hooked rugs instead of carpets. The need to transport produce led to a wide variety of baskets; basketry skills were passed on from generation to generation. The Puritans' "moral distrust of the ornate" did not extend to the utilitarian world of household objects, where handiwork was valued as an important outlet for creativity. Also, the work ethic has been so deeply ingrained in the Yankee temperament that diaries and other domestic papers from early Vermonters testify to the imperative "to be busy and avoid idleness." ❧

Sampler Quilt by Jane A. Stickle, 1863. This heroically sized quilt, nearly seven feet on a side, contains 5,602 pieces and bears the sewn inscription "In War Time." *Bennington Museum. Below: Market Basket* by Cemore Landon Morehouse, c. late 19th century. The body of this basket is handmade, with a mass-produced wire swing handle. *Shelburne Museum*

How to Make a Basket

"YOU GET A LOG, BRING IT HOME, PEEL THE BARK, and throw the bark away. The rest of the log you use. You beat the whole length of the log with a hammer to get strips off it. One year's growth to a time. Then you split it in whatever widths you're going to be using. To make it smooth you shave it on both sides with a knife and a leather on your leg. And go ahead and make your basket."

Newton Washburn, basketmaker, born 1915

The Webb family at Shelburne Farms, in a family photograph, 1916. The estate now hosts a nonprofit education center, a palatial inn, and summer concerts. *Shelburne Museum Opposite above:* The gardens at Hildene, in Manchester, were created in 1903. *Photo The Hildene Archive. Opposite below:* The Currier residence at Currier Farms, Danby, 1959. Vermont landscape architect Dan Kiley has won renown for his artful syntheses of modernist design principles, formal geometric elements, traditional rural forms, and vernacular materials. This design incorporates locally quarried marble and spring water from the nearby woods channeled through the property in a nod to mogul garden tradition. *Office of Dan Kiley*

Generous Gardens

Vermont's relative inaccessibility, brief growing season, and pervasive democratic spirit proved inhospitable to grand estate gardens attached to grand houses. The exceptions are all the more striking. Robert Todd Lincoln, the president's son, established Hildene, a 24-room Georgian Revival mansion in Manchester that included formal gardens, now open to the public. More elaborate still is Shelburne Farms, created by Vanderbilt heiress Lila Webb, overlooking Lake Champlain. Shelburne was "back to nature" on a grand scale: its landscape and model farm were designed by renowned forester Gifford Pinchot, who consulted with Frederick Law Olmsted. The site now includes a working farm and partially restored gardens. Vermont gardeners today create beauty and exceptional produce during a growing season of just 90 days. The revival in growing heirloom vegetables is strong here; there's a well-known demonstration garden in Burlington. Heritage roses are displayed in East Craftsbury, wildflowers at a Charlotte farm; an outdoor flower festival is held annually in Stowe.

"[I REMEMBER] LUGGING THOSE LITTLE MEN TO THE LAUNDRY building every fall and fetchin' 'em back again every spring."

Henry Noonan, age 85, gardener at Shelburne Farms, on the upkeep of its grand Italian gardens with their Venetian stone sculptures, 1988

VERMONT VICTUALS

Right: A root vegetable pie from Chelsea United Church. *Photo Lisa Charles Watson. Below:* Ben & Jerry's snazzy blend of can-do capitalism and civic-mindedness has been a hit with the boomer generation, who also delighted in product names such as Cherry Garcia, Wavy Gravy, Doonesberry, Peace Pops, and Rainforest Crunch. Its factory is the premier tourist attraction in the state, offering daily tours. *Packaging and product names © 1998 Ben & Jerry's Homemade Holdings, Inc. Used with permission*

From earliest days, local game and produce dominated Vermont menus. Typical meals might include venison (fresh or smoked), partridge, bear steak, trout, squirrel stew, wood-pigeon pie, cornmeal mush, and baked beans. Even porcupines and groundhogs were hunted for food in hard times. Wild berries and greens were plentiful, and cooks used maple sugar or syrup as an all-purpose flavoring. Vermont fare is still hearty—an American Legion fundraiser offers ten varieties of wild game—with touches of an upscale sensibility awakened in the summer resorts and ski belt. Pancakes, onto which maple syrup goes perfectly, and from which calories are available for battling the winter cold, are staples at the many diners and pancake houses statewide. Ben Cohen and Jerry Greenfield founded their ice cream empire in Burlington in 1978, capitalizing as much on Vermont ideals as on Vermont cows. The company churns a percentage of its profits into good causes. ❧

Chicken Supper Chicken Pie

To make the chicken: boil until tender. Remove all skin and bones. Discard gizzard, heart, and liver. Thicken enough broth to make a sauce and add chicken cut into small pieces. Salt and pepper to taste. Keep hot. To make the biscuits:

> 2 tbsp. shortening
> 2 cups flour
> 1 tsp. salt
> 4 tsp. baking powder
> About ¾ cup milk

Cut shortening into dry ingredients. Add enough milk so you can handle it on a board. Roll out to about one inch thick. Cut out rounds with biscuit cutter. Then put boiling hot chicken and gravy into a baking dish and put biscuits all over the top. Bake at 400° F until biscuits are done, about ½ hour. Test by raising one biscuit in the middle.

"YEARS AGO PEOPLE PUT UP BARRELS OF SALTED smelt caught in the spawning season, bins of root vegetables, canned green tomatoes, and grated horseradish cut with turnip. Then in midwinter, after letting a barrel of hard cider freeze, they'd drill a hole in the middle and tap the nearly pure alcohol, which made a man's heart feel as if it were wrapped in soft cotton."

Edward Hoagland, Walking the Dead Diamond River, *1973*

Chicken Pie Supper by Hilda Belcher, 1937. Belcher's work shows the influence of Ashcan School painters George Bellows and Robert Henri, her contemporaries. *Robert Hull Fleming Museum*

Ice Fishing on Lake Willoughby by Stephen Huneck, 1987. Contemporary folk artist Huneck left art school to work in a lumber mill and later gained renown for the sophisticated charm of his wood carvings and paintings, many depicting animals. Here he shows the gamut of Vermont winter pursuits, arranging figures and landscape into a decorative pattern. *Stephen Huneck Gallery, Woodstock. Below: Loon* by Earl Cheney, 1981. Cheney, of Newport, has been carving wood decoys since age 12. *Erik Borg/Vermont Folklife Center*

Vermonters celebrate their rustic roots with fairs, roundups, festivals, field days, workshops, concerts, bakeoffs, auctions, and derbies. Lacking a major-league sports franchise, residents loyally support their high school football teams. Contrary to the popular image, warm-weather sports such as bicycling, hiking, backpacking, golfing, kayaking, and tennis are more important to the economy than winter sports; Vermont has more tennis courts per capita than any other state, and many

ski areas are now promoted as all-weather resorts. For hunters, the wilderness is as wild and remote as one could wish, and game has made a comeback. Fisherfolk flock to streams and lakes, practicing their sport year-round. Antiquing is integral to the fabric of life—so much so, says Vermont historian Charles Morrissey, that Vermont "is like one huge antique shop." Desirable local items include tools related to the maple sugar industry, blacksmithing and farm implements, tinware, pewter, Bennington pottery, and firearms. ❦

Kayaking in one of Vermont's rivers. *Photo Richard Smith/Corbis Below:* Triathlon swimmers in Lake Champlain. *Photo Phil Schermeister/ Corbis*

"ALL VERMONTERS HUNTED and fished and, what was worse, talked about it."

Norman Rockwell, My Adventures as an Illustrator, *1960*

"There's always snow in Stowe."

Vermont saying

White Gold

Local enthusiasts created Vermont's first ski areas early in the 20th century; few outsiders ventured onto the slopes. Then came the nation's first ski lift—in Woodstock in 1934—priming the pump for what is now a $750 million annual industry. Vermont ranks third nationally in the number of skier days, with 4 million, outstripped only by Colorado and California. The state's 21 Alpine resorts comprise more than 1,000 trails on 5,500 acres of skiable terrain. Major resorts—the so-called Gold Towns—include Stowe, Bolton Valley, Jay Peak, Mad River Glen, Sugarbush, and Smugglers' Notch in the north; Killington, Suicide Six, and Okemo in the middle; and Stratton, Mount Snow, Ascutney, Bromley,

The Vermont Life

Since 1946 *Vermont Life* magazine has promoted the state's seasonal joys to an avid audience. "Vermont is a way of life" was its original slogan; its first publisher was the Vermont State Development Commission. But the magazine achieved more than mere flackery. Thanks to enlightened editors, it has consistently attracted superior writing and photography. It pioneered the pictorial spread and created a distinctive voice through such features as "Green Mountain Postboy."

Heading North by Ann Coleman, 1997. *Courtesy the artist. Opposite above:* Cover of *Vermont Life* magazine, winter 1988. *Opposite below:* Cover of a souvenir program for Winter Carnival in Burlington, 1887. Vermont towns such as Burlington, Rutland, Montpelier, and St. Johnsbury began promoting themselves as winter destinations as early as the 1880s. "Winter Carnivals" featured snowshoeing, toboggan rides, skating, ice boating, and hockey games. *Special Collections, University of Vermont*

and Magic Mountain in the south. Outside the ski resorts, and less quantifiable by numbers, cross-country skiers, snowmobilers, snowshoers, dog sledders, and ice fishers find plenty of space—and white stuff—in which to pursue their passions.

A Writer's Landscape

Vermont's first presses were established a dozen years before statehood, and were immediately put to good use. Ethan Allen and his brother Ira published pamphlets to urge fellow settlers to forge an independent republic, and Colonial dramatist Loyall Tyler wrote the first comedy to be performed on an American stage. Since then, Vermont has attracted writers as diverse as Rudyard Kipling, who wrote his "Just So" stories near Brattleboro, and Sinclair Lewis, whose *It Can't Happen Here* imagined the fascist takeover of a fictional Vermont town. Writers may come on holiday, or to attend the Bread Loaf Writers' Conference, and stay because of the state's quiet beauty—and its proximity to Boston and New York. Alexander Solzhenitzyn lived in Vermont during his years of exile from Russia;

Sinclair Lewis and Dorothy Thompson in 1928, the year the two writers married and bought their Twin Farms property in Barnard. It's now an inn with some Lewis memorabilia on display. *Culver Pictures. Right: Alexander Isayevich Solzhenitsyn* by James Gill, 1968. From a *Time* magazine cover, September 27, 1968. *National Portrait Gallery/ Time, Inc.*

novelist John Irving lives and teaches in southern Vermont. Urban refugees in residence have included novelist Jamaica Kincaid, playwright David Mamet, and poets Galway Kinnell and Hayden Carruth. Dorothy Canfield Fisher, Vermont's "First Lady of Letters," for years supplied books to her good friend and Arlington neighbor, the painter Norman Rockwell.

The Falls

The elemental murmur
as they plunge, *croal, croal,*
and *haish, haish,* over
the ledges,
through stepless wheels
and bare axles, down between
sawmills that have
buckled and slid sideways to their knees...

When I fall I would fall to my sounding...
the lowly,
unchanged, stillic, rainbowed sounding
of the Barton River Falls.

Galway Kinnell, from Body Rags, *1968*

...we are still here, although we're passing on.
You won't hear much about us, but we're here.
I think we are the last true regionalists,
or maybe—who knows?—the first of a new breed.
Not local colorists, at any rate, not keepers
of quaintness for quaintness's sake. We're realists.

Hayden Carruth, from "Vermont," in
Brothers, I Loved You All, *1978*

Scratchboard drawing by Michael McCurdy of the home of writer Edward Hoagland in Barton, 1997. Hoagland is a much-admired nature essayist whose books include *Red Wolves and Black Bears. Courtesy the artist*

"I had a lover's quarrel with the world."

Inscription on Frost's tombstone in Bennington

Robert Frost. Photograph by Clara Sipprell, c. 1962. *University of Vermont Opposite above:* Frost's cabin in Ripton. *Photo Orah Moore. Opposite below:* Frost's Morris chair and lapboard. *Middlebury College*

Robert Frost (1874–1963) is so closely identified with Vermont that it seems incongruous that he was born in San Francisco. In 1939, Frost bought a farm in Ripton, near Middlebury College ("Not so near I know it's there"), and he took an early interst in the Bread Loaf Writers' Conference as "a place in Vermont where a writer can try his effect on readers." Bread Loaf still conducts a major summer writing program. Vermont claimed Frost for posterity by naming him poet laureate in 1962, a year before his death. A year earlier Frost had enthralled Americans by reading one of his poems at John F. Kennedy's inauguration.

Frost took his inspiration from the land and people around him, writing conversationally about seemingly mundane matters. Among his best-known poems are "Stopping by Woods on a Snowy Evening," "The Road Not Taken," and "Mending Wall." By all accounts a difficult man, he left an indelible mark on the nation's literary life and remains its best-loved poet. ❦

The Pasture

I'm going out to clean the pasture spring;
I'll only stop to rake the leaves away
(And wait to watch the water clear, I may):
I sha'n't be gone long.—You come too.

I'm going out to fetch the little calf
That's standing by the mother. It's so young
It totters when she licks it with her tongue.
I sha'n't be gone long.—You come too.

Dedicated by the poet to his wife, Elinor

Breathes there a bard who isn't moved
When he finds his verse is understood
And not entirely disapproved
By his country and his neighborhood?

"On Being Chosen Poet of Vermont"
Robert Frost in 1961, at Stowe

Why do you talk so much
Robert Frost? One day
I drove up to Ripton to ask,

I stayed the whole day
And never got the chance
To put the
question.

I drove off at dusk
Worn out and aching
In both ears....

Galway Kinnell,
from "For Robert Frost," 1964

Show Business, Vermont Style

Alfred Hitchcock was the first filmmaker to exploit Vermont's scenic potential when he had a corpse pop up amid the crisp autumn leaves of Craftsbury Common in *The Trouble with Harry*. A handful of other movies *(Ethan Frome, The Spitfire Grill, Baby Boom)* have used Green Mountain landscapes as background, but Vermont has not courted Hollywood as some states have.

Performance art thrives, led by two only-in-Vermont arts groups. Catamount Arts in the Northeast Kingdom has brought film, theater, and dance experiences to tiny towns without proper stages. And the influential Bread and Puppet Theater, a troupe of audacious city refugees, powerfully synthesizes visual art, drama, and ideology. Every year Bread and Puppet stages a two-day drama in the forests outside Glover with monstrously sized puppets that symbolize the political outrage of the moment. A museum in Glover exhibits its past creations.

You and I and moon-light in Ver - mont.

Musical Traditions

Austria's von Trapp family knew Vermont had a song in its heart: when the *Sound of Music* clan fled Nazi rule, they landed in the hills of Stowe and opened the Trapp Family Lodge. Vermont enjoys musical expressions from hymn and shape-note singing, inside and outside of churches, to the rock group Phish, which sprang from a Burlington bar. Clogging, fiddling, and folk dancing are resurgent; the melodies and rhythms of French Canada filter down from Quebec. Contemporary folk music can be heard at fairs, in coffeehouses, and each August at the Champlain Valley Festival. Notable in the classical world are composer Carl Ruggles (also a painter), and the Marlboro Music Festival (founded by the conductor Rudolf Serkin). Old theaters around the state—most notably

the art deco Flynn in Burlington and the Barre Opera House—have undergone extensive restoration and now showcase dance, theater, and music companies, including the Vermont Symphony Orchestra.

Above left: Since 1944, "Moonlight in Vermont" has been recorded by more than 200 artists, among them Frank Sinatra, Sarah Vaughn, Ray Charles, and Willie Nelson. *Above:* The Bing Crosby vehicle *White Christmas* portrayed an idyllic Vermont but was really filmed in California. *Photofest. Left:* Maria von Trapp and her brother Johannes at the lodge, 1998. *Photo Sandy Macys/ The New York Times*

The art of Grandma Moses was first exhibited professionally in 1939 in the show "Unknown American Painters" at the Museum of Modern Art in New York. *Above:* Moses on her 101st birthday, photograph by Otto Kallir. *Right: Christmas at Home, 1946. All images these pages © Grandma Moses Properties Co., New York*

The celebrated primitive painter Grandma Moses (1860–1961) was born Anna Mary Robertson in New York State, within shouting distance of the Vermont border. She took up painting at age 67 after her husband died, using cheap brushes and house paint to produce whimsical scenes of country life remembered from her childhood. Her subjects were the stuff of rural social life—quilting bees, barn dances, sugar mapling, holiday homecomings—all rendered in minute detail. When an art collector saw her paintings at a local drugstore he took her

under his wing, providing her with materials and putting her in touch with museums and dealers. After her work was first exhibited in 1939, her career was launched. Moses's homespun works struck a comforting chord during the war years, and were among the first artistic works to be licensed for greeting cards and other commercial products. Today much of her work resides at the Bennington Museum, providing inspiration to generations of untrained artists. ✤

In the Park, 1944. In this pastoral scene, figures cross a covered bridge on a path leading to the distant Bennington Battle Monument. Moses lived in Bennington for two years, and much of her work resides in its museum.

Sugaring Off by Grandma Moses, 1955. All images these pages © *Grandma Moses Properties Co., New York*

"AS FAR AS I KNOW SHE NEVER PAINTED ANYTHING UP TO DATE. A car became a buggy; a tractor, a team of horses....The world of her childhood is more vivid and real to her than the modern world. All the years have not effaced it."

Norman Rockwell on Grandma Moses, in My Adventures as an Illustrator, *1960*

Grandma Moses's response to the question, "How do you paint?" was typically down-to-earth:

"Before I start painting I get a frame, then I saw my masonite board to fit the frame."

Grandma Moses: My Life's History, *1952*

Below: Battle of Bennington (1953) was commissioned by the Daughters of the American Revolution. In it Moses depicted the battle as well as the monument erected years later to commemorate it. *Right:* The Grandma Moses stamp was issued on May 1, 1969, to mark the beginning of Senior Citizens' Month. It reproduces a detail of Moses's *July Fourth,* appropriately owned by the White House.

Artists are at work in studios all over the state, in every kind of medium and style. Regional showcases, such as the Helen Day Art Center in Stowe and the Southern Vermont Art Center in Manchester, mount changing exhibits of Vermont-based artists. Perhaps the strongest trend, though, is the revival

of folk arts and fine crafts, which draws on a long legacy of handmade objects. Today the farming tradition reveals itself in an intense interest in needlework, especially quilting, knitting, rug hooking, and braiding. The logging camps of the 19th century gave rise to wood crafts, and these too are enjoying a resurgence via practitioners who whittle, paint, build miniatures, and create contemporary updates of

A Heart Like Mexican Weather by Jim Dine, 1998. *Pace Wildenstein Gallery, New York. Photo Gordon Riley Christmas. Below: Lab Throne* by Stephen Huneck, 1994. *Stephen Huneck Gallery, Woodstock. Opposite above:* The Raimbillis, a life-size fantasy family of 24, with artist Gayleen Aiken. Aiken's work was discovered by Grass Roots Art and Community Effort (GRACE), which develops and promotes self-taught artists in rural Vermont. *Photo Gail Mooney. Opposite below:* Wood-fired stoneware bowl by Karen Karnes, c. 1990s. *Courtesy the artist*

the fantailed birds once turned out by loggers. The art of woven basketry has been fostered by an apprenticeship program at the Vermont Folklife Center, the state's most active sponsor of folk art; here old-timers pass on Abenaki basketry skills, and Southeast Asian immigrants teach floral arranging to newly inspired crafters. ❧

A Sense of Place

Vermont's natural beauty has inspired an aesthetic
based on trees, hills, nature, and light. Love of the land
itself has influenced contemporary Vermont artists—
not just those who paint landscapes, like Wolf Kahn,
but also those who use the land itself in their work.
Painter Francis Hewitt moved from hard-edge abstrac-
tion to a "dirt" series that displayed actual soil from
the four corners of the state. Although commercial
galleries and contemporary museums are few, the land
itself becomes a gallery in some artists' work. Landscape architect Dan Kiley has built an international

reputation blending vernacular materials with classical forms. In addition, site-specific work is thriving in the central and southern part of the state. One such undertaking, called the Hay Art Project and staged at Shelburne Farms, brought together several artists from different disciplines to explore the meaning of hayfields and haystacks to present-day Vermonters.

Above: Zeus by Chuck Ginnever, 1975. *Collection the artist. Left: Vermont Flag* by Francis Hewitt, 1989. In the 1960s, abstractionist Hewitt moved from New York, where he was a member of the Anonima Group, to East Corinth, Vermont. Some of his paintings incorporate Vermont earth. *Institute for Progressive Painting. Photo Ken Burris. Opposite above: Trees Changing Color* by Wolf Kahn, 1996. *Courtesy the artist. Opposite below:* Taoist talisman mowed into a hayfield by artists Knox Cummin and Bill Botzow, part of the "Hay Art" project. *Photo Toby Talbot/AP*

Take the Green Train

The Green Mountain Flyer is one of several seasonal excursion trains that ply Vermont's scenic corridors. The Flyer originates in Bellows Falls; its restored coaches, pulled by vintage diesels, cruise along the Connecticut and Williams Rivers and cross two covered bridges en route to Chester Depot. Historic train stations are still in use (or adaptive reuse) around the state.

Heavenly Stone

Barre (pronounced *Barry*) lies at the heart of Vermont's granite industry, with quarries like this one supplying stone for buildings nationwide. Barre's cemeteries, called Hope and Elmwood, are showcases for granite stonework. Fine examples repose here from many periods and carvers. Not far away, in Proctor, is the Vermont Marble Exhibit, the world's largest display on marble history.

Baited Breath

The American Museum of Fly Fishing in Manchester is a fishing enthusiast's fish heaven. In addition to housing a 2,500-volume library devoted just to books on fishing, the museum exhibits the tackles of celebrities as diverse as Winslow Homer, Daniel Webster, and Bing Crosby—all devotees of the sport.

Major Scoop

An ice cream parlor to rival Disneyland? Ben & Jerry's headquarters in Waterbury, near Burlington, offers factory tours, ice cream tastings, rides, multimedia presentations, and places to picnic. It's the number one destination in the state. When they're not mixing up new flavors or conquering new markets, company employees chill out in predictable ways: like creating the world's largest ice cream sculpture.

Blooming Natives

The Vermont Wildflower Farm in Charlotte (just down the road from Burlington and Shelburne) is the largest producer of wildflower seed in the East. They ship seed all over the country to those who want to cultivate their own flowery meadows and woodlands. The farm staff helps visitors create their own combinations or choose a preblended mixture.

Beached Inland

Whales in Vermont? Prehistorically, of course. In their honor and as a tribute to the state's environmental sympathies, a remarkable sculpture called *Whales' Tails/ Reverence* rises from a pasture near I-89 at the Randolph exit. The two enormous, curving whale tails, made of African granite, are the work of Randolph-based sculptor Jim Sardonis.

Great People

A selective listing of Vermonters, native and adopted, concentrating on the arts.

Thomas Waterman Wood
(1823–1903), 19th-century painter
of Vermont scenes

George D. Aiken (1892–1984),
governor and U.S. senator,
coined the name Northeast
Kingdom

Ethan Allen (1738–1789), patriot,
leader of Green Mountain Boys

Warren Austin (1877–1962), U.S.
senator, first U.S. representative
to the UN

Hilda Belcher (1881–1963),
portrait and genre painter

W. A. Bentley (1865–1931),
farmer and photographer,
called the Snowflake King

Daniel J. Cady (1861–1934),
Vermont poet ("It beats a day
on Woodstock Green.")

Thomas Chittenden (1730–1797),
Vermont's first governor

Calvin Coolidge (1872–1933),
"Silent Cal," 30th president, first
to speak on the radio

Thomas Royal Dake (1786–1852),
early 19th-century architect

John Deere (1804–1866), blacksmith and inventor of the first
successful steel plow

John Dewey (1859–1952), philos-
opher, writer, educational
reformer; born in Burlington

Dorothy Canfield Fisher
(1879–1958), novelist and essayist
who "interpreted" Vermont

Frances Frost (1905–1959), poet
(unrelated to Robert Frost)

Robert Frost (1874–1963),
Pulitzer Prize–winning poet;
lived most of his life in Vermont; named its poet laureate

Henry Oscar Houghton
(1823–1895), founder of the publishing house Houghton Mifflin

Richard Morris Hunt
(1827–1895), architect, born in
Brattleboro; designed many
New York landmarks

Sinclair Lewis (1885–1951), Nobel
Prize–winning novelist

Larkin Mead (1835–1910), sculptor and illustrator

Justin Smith Morrill (1810–1898),
U.S. senator; established land
grant colleges

Redfield Proctor (1831–1908),
marble tycoon and politician

Rowland Evans Robinson
(1833–1900), writer and illustrator
of folksy Vermont tales

Carl Ruggles (1876–1971),
composer and painter

Rudolf Serkin (1903–1991),
pianist; longtime director of
Marlboro Music Festival

Joseph Smith (1805–1844), and
Brigham Young (1801–1877),
founders of Mormon Church

Rudy Vallee (1901–1986),
crooner and movie star; born
in Island Pond

...and Great Places

Some interesting derivations of Vermont place names.

Barre Originally named Wildersburgh in 1780, then renamed in 1793. Of two possibilities, Captain Joseph Thompson backed Holden, his former home in Massachusetts; Jonathan Sherman backed Barre. Sherman won—literally in a brawl on a barn floor.

Bennington Named for New Hampshire governor Benning Wentworth, who donated land to Dartmouth College.

Caledonia County Named for the former name of Scotland.

Chittenden County For Thomas Chittenden, first governor of the colonial assembly and territorial governor of Vermont.

Franklin Named for Benjamin Franklin.

Glastenbury Near Shaftsbury and presumably named (if misspelled) for the English town that figures in Arthurian legend, it thrived in the 1830s but is now a ghost town.

Guildhall In far northern Vermont on the Connecticut River; claims to be the only town in the world with this name.

Irasburg In honor of Ira Allen, brother of Ethan Allen.

Jay In honor of 18th-century statesman John Jay.

Lamoille County The name is a corruption of La Mouette, the name that Samuel de Champlain gave to the river.

Lemon Fair River A Vermonter's attempt to render Les Monts Verts, the original French designation for Vermont.

Milton Named after the immortal poet John Milton.

Montpelier The capital's name comes from the French town Montpellier (*mont*, hill; *peler*, to strip or make bald).

Moscow Imaginatively named by someone who thought that a large saw blade sounded like church bells in Moscow.

Smugglers' Notch As the name implies, this was where some Americans smuggled supplies to the British during the War of 1812.

St. Johnsbury Christened in honor of Hector St. Jean de Crevcoeur with the Anglicized form of his name.

Washington County With Montpelier as its seat, it was named for George Washington.

Winooski A town and a river, from the Indian word for "onion." The river used to be called the Onion River.

Marlboro Named for England's Duke of Marlborough.

VERMONT BY THE SEASONS
A Perennial Calendar of Events and Festivals

*Here is a selective listing of events that take place each year in the months noted;
we suggest calling ahead to local chambers of commerce for dates and details.
Most ski resorts hold winter events during snow season.*

January

Brookfield
Ice Harvest Festival
Demonstrations and competitions.

East Burke
White Out Days Winter Carnival
Big Air Snowboarding Competition

Jeffersonville
Winterfest
Primitive biathlon, cross-country race, sleigh rides, fireworks.

Stowe
Winter Carnival
A week of ski races and entertainment.

Whitingham
Harriman Ice Fishing Derby

February

Brattleboro
Ski Touring Race
Country's oldest race tour.
Winter Carnival

Burlington
Waltz Night and Silent Auction
Fundraiser for Vermont Symphony Orchestra.
Winter Festival
Magic Hat Mardi Gras Parade

Fair Haven
Valentine's Chicken Pie Supper

Huntington
Owl Walk
Experience winter's night vocalists at Green Mountain Audubon Nature Center.

Norwich
Igloo Build
Build igloo village; dependent on snow cover.

March

East Burke
Annual Pond Skimming
At Burke Mountain Resort.

Essex Junction
Whisk Away Weekend: An Italian Culinary Experience

Fair Haven
St. Patrick's Corned Beef Supper

Middlebury
Middlebury College Winter Carnival

Montpelier
Farmers' Night
Free Vermont Symphony Orchestra concert.

Various locations
Sugar-on-snow and maple festivals in many towns.

April

Dummerston Center
Baked Ham and Bean Supper

Rutland
Festival of Quilts

Various locations
Maple festivals in Franklin County, St. Albans, elsewhere.

May

Statewide
Craft Open Studios Weekend
On Memorial Day weekend.
Abenaki Cultural Heritage Week

Quechee
Covered Bridges Half-Marathon
Starts at Suicide Six, Woodstock; ends at Queechee Polo Field.

Shelburne
Lilac Festival
Family activities and music.

Woodstock
Spring Farm Festival

June

Burlington
Discover Jazz Festival
Weeklong concerts featuring international artists.

Enosburg Falls
Dairy Festival

Manchester
Antique and Classic Car Show
Major vintage car event at
Hildene Meadowlands.

Sugarbush Resort
Ben & Jerry's One World Festival
Company's annual board meeting has blossomed into a festival
with music, political action,
and, of course, ice cream.

Sunderland
Ethan Allen Days
Battle reenactments, period
crafters, camp tours.

Woodstock
Heirloom Seed Day
Hand-Milking Contest
Both at Billings Farm and
Museum, which sponsors farm-related activities year-round.

July

Barton
Vermont Forestry Expo
Lumberjack Roundup, truck
rodeo, log rolling; at Barton
Fairgrounds.

Basin Harbor
Lake Champlain Small Boat Show

Marlboro
Marlboro Music Festival
Concerts in July and August.

Northfield
Slavic Festival
Folk dancing, choral singing,
poetry, theater performances.
Solzhenitsyn once came.

Vermont Quilt Festival

North Hero
Antique Show and Sale
Hermann's Royal Lipizzan Stallions
Equestrian ballet; a group of the
famous horses has a permament
summer home here.

Putney
Yellow Barn Music Festival
Concerts, master classes, suppers;
five weeks in July and August.

August

Bennington
Bennington Battle Weekend
Parade, reenactments, artillery
display around a state holiday.

Essex Junction
Champlain Valley Fair
Vermont's largest fair.

Glover
*Bread and Puppet Theater Domestic
Resurrection Circus*
Two-day event in the pastures
draws thousands.

Lyndonville
Dowsing School and Convention
Workshops teach basic dowsing.

September

Statewide
Vermont Archeology Week
Events at several locations
include atlatl-throwing.

Rutland
Vermont State Fair

Stratton
Stratton Arts Festival
Arts and crafts, performances;
to mid-October.

Tunbridge
World's Fair
Three-day event includes pony
pulling, rodeo, oxen judging.

Various locations
Harvest Festivals, Apple Days
*Northeast Kingdom Fall Foliage
Festival*
In seven towns.

October

Killington
Sheep and Wool Festival
Sheep-shearing demonstrations,
sheep dog handling.

Weston
Antiques Show
One of the best in the state.

Woodstock
Apple and Crafts Fair

November

Bradford
Wild Game Supper
Menu includes bear, venison,
pheasant, rabbit, and moose.

December

Bennington
Museum Week

Manchester
Scottish Winter Ball
Gala fund-raiser and dinner
dance at the Equinox Hotel.

Candlelight Tours
At Hildene: sleigh/wagon rides,
music, decorations, tours.

Woodstock
Wassail Christmas Festival

WHERE TO GO
Museums, Attractions, Gardens, and Other Arts Resources

Call for seasons and hours when open.

Museums

AMERICAN PRECISION MUSEUM
Windsor, 802-674-5781
Large collection of historically significant machine tools housed in original National Historic Landmark building.

ATHENAEUM ART GALLERY AND LIBRARY
St. Johnsbury, 802-748-8291
Oldest unaltered art gallery of its type in National Historic Landmark site shows works from the Hudson River School.

BENNINGTON MUSEUM
W. Main St., Bennington, 802-447-1571
Bennington pottery, glass, furniture, decorative arts, tools, toys, military artifacts, and Grandma Moses paintings.

BILLINGS FARM AND MUSEUM
Rt. 12, Woodstock, 802-457-2355
Agricultural museum and dairy farm features a working farm, restored farmhouse, and extensive farm life exhibits.

BRATTLEBORO MUSEUM AND ART CENTER
Union Station, Main and Vernon Sts., 802-257-0124
Rotating exhibits on traditional and contemporary art, plus display of Estey Organs and company history.

BREAD AND PUPPET MUSEUM
Rt. 122, Glover, 802-525-3031
Masks and puppets from noted theater troupe displayed in 128-year-old barn.

FAIRBANKS MUSEUM AND PLANETARIUM
Main St., St. Johnsbury, 802-748-2372
Victorian building houses exhibits on animals, tools, toys, dolls, dinosaurs, and rural history, and a U.S. weather broadcast station.

LAKE CHAMPLAIN MARITIME MUSEUM
Off Basin Harbor Rd., Basin Harbor, 802-475-2022
Historical exhibits of Lake Champlain, including a full-size working replica of Benedict Arnold's gunboat.

OLD STONE HOUSE MUSEUM
Brownington, 802-754-2022.
Granite structure built in 1836 by Alexander Twilight as a dormitory now houses exhibits mounted by the Orleans Historical Society.

PORTER MUSIC BOX MUSEUM
Randolph, 800-635-1938
Extensive collection of large antique music boxes, musical automata, and a reproducing piano.

ROBERT HULL FLEMING MUSEUM
UVM, 61 Colchester Ave., Burlington, 802-656-0750
Art and anthropology museum features paintings, sculpture, prints, drawings, and decorative arts with a Vermont focus.

SHELDON MUSEUM
1 Park St., Middlebury, 802-88-2117
Furniture, portraits; also rotating exhibits.

SHELBURNE MUSEUM
Rt. 7, Shelburne, 802-985-3346
Thirty-seven buildings on 45 acres house 80,000 historical objects, plus the steamship Ticonderoga.

T. W. WOOD GALLERY
Vermont College, Montpelier, 802-828-8743
Contemporary exhibits and permanent collection of Thomas Waterman Wood and other artists of the 1920s and 30s.

VERMONT HISTORICAL SOCIETY
Montpelier, 802-828-2291
Rotating thematic exhibits relating to Vermont's past.

Attractions

BEN & JERRY'S ICE CREAM FACTORY TOURS
Rt. 100, Waterbury, 802-244-TOUR
Free tastings on weekdays.

BENNINGTON BATTLE MONUMENT
Off Vt. 9, Bennington, 802-447-0550
The tallest structure in Vermont, 306 feet high.

CHIMNEY POINT STATE HISTORIC SITE
Rts. 17 and 125 at the Champlain Bridge, Addison,
802-759-2412
Interpretive exhibit provides an overview of Native Americans and French settlement in the Champlain Valley.

CROWLEY CHEESE FACTORY
Healdville, 802-259-2340
National Historic Place shows cheese being made by hand as it was in the 19th century.

HUBBARDTON BATTLEFIELD AND MUSEUM
7 miles off U.S. 4, East Hubbardton, 802-273-2282
Site of Revolutionary War battle, with interpretive exhibit.

NEW ENGLAND MAPLE MUSEUM & MAPLE MARKET
U.S. 7, Pittsford, 802-483-9414
Complete exhibit on maple sugaring from sap to syrup.

OLD CONSTITUTION HOUSE
U.S. 5, Windsor, 802-674-6628
Restored tavern where delegates met in 1777 to create the Republic of Vermont; exhibit on Vermont constitution.

ROBERT FROST INTERPRETIVE TRAIL
Ripton, 802-388-4362
Frost poems and interpretive information mounted on plaques along .3-mile hiking trail.

ROCK OF AGES GRANITE QUARRIES
Barre, 802-476-3119
Self-guided quarry tours show cutting, sculpting, polishing.

ST. ANNE'S SHRINE
Isle La Motte, 802-928-3362
Religious and historical site with statue of Champlain.

SHELBURNE FARMS
Harbor and Bay Rds., Shelburne, 802-985-8686
Working farm on 1,400-acre National Historic property on Lake Champlain.

UNDERWATER HISTORIC PRESERVES
Five sites in Lake Champlain, accessible to scuba divers.

UVM MORGAN HORSE FARM
Weybridge, 802-388-2011
Working farm, guided tours, video show.

VERMONT MARBLE EXHIBIT
62 Main St. Proctor, 802-459-2300
Historical exhibit of marble industry.

VERMONT TEDDY BEAR COMPANY
Rt. 7, Shelburne Rd., Shelburne, 802-985-1322
Factory tour shows how a teddy bear is made.

Homes and Gardens

ETHAN ALLEN HOMESTEAD
Off Rt. 127, Burlington, 802-865-4556
Restored 1787 farmhouse includes multimedia show and exhibits about Allen and the Green Mountain Boys.

HILDENE
Rt. 7A, Manchester Village, 802-447-1571
Georgian Revival mansion built by Robert Todd Lincoln exhibits original furnishings and family effects as well as formal gardens and a working 1908 Aeolian organ.

HISTORIC GRAFTON VILLAGE
Rts. 121 and 35, Grafton, 802-843-2584
Restored 19th-century community; one of the finest examples of rural New England village life.

HYDE LOG CABIN
U.S. 2, Grand Isle, 802-372-5440
One of the oldest log cabins in the U.S., built in 1783 and furnished with historical items.

THE JOHN STRONG MANSION
Near Crown Point Bridge, Addison, 802-759-2309
Colonial Herb Garden and period furnishings in a restored mansion originally built in 1796.

JOSEPH SMITH BIRTHPLACE MEMORIAL
Sharon & South Royalton, 802-763-7742
One of the world's largest granite shafts marks the birthplace of the Mormon founder.

JUSTIN SMITH MORRILL HOMESTEAD
Justin Morrill Hwy., Strafford, 802-765-4484
Gothic Revival mansion and furnishings from the 1840s.

PARK-McCULLOUGH HOUSE MUSEUM
Off Rt. 67A, North Bennington, 802-442-5441
Historic Victorian mansion exhibits personal belongings, furnishings, and papers of several generations of noted Vermont families. Estate includes carriage barn, children's playhouse, and formal gardens.

PLYMOUTH NOTCH
Rt. 100A, Plymouth Notch, 802-672-3773
President Calvin Coolidge State Historic Site includes birthplace, boyhood home, and burial place.

VERMONT WILDFLOWER FARM
Rt. 7, Shelburne, 802-425-3500
Six acres of wildflowers from all regions of the country.

WILSON CASTLE
Off Rt. 4 on the West Proctor Road, Rutland, 802-773-3284
Mid-19th century mansion with European and Far Eastern furnishings on a 115-acre estate.

Other Resources

BENNINGTON CENTER FOR THE ARTS
Rt. 9W, at Gypsy Lane, 802-442-7158
Home of Vermont's largest annual art exhibits and sales, juried exhibits, and performances.

BRIGGS OPERA HOUSE
White River Junction, 802-295-5432
Ongoing performances of music, dance, and theater.

CATAMOUNT ARTS
60 Eastern Ave., St. Johnsbury, 802-748-2600
Music, dance, theater performances, film screenings, gallery, and art classes.

HELEN DAY ART CENTER
School St., Stowe, 802-253-8358
Contemporary art exhibits, lectures, and classes.

NORMAN ROCKWELL EXHIBITION
Main St., Arlington, 802-375-6423
Saturday Evening Post covers, illustrations, advertisements, and prints exhibited in the town where Rockwell lived.

SOUTHERN VERMONT ART CENTER
West Rd., Manchester, 802-362-1405
Galleries, sculpture garden, and rotating exhibits of contemporary art housed in a National Historic Trust mansion.

STATE HOUSE
115 State St., Montpelier, 802-828-2228
Recently restored Greek Revival building of Barre granite, in use since 1859.

VERMONT STATE CRAFT CENTER AT FROG HOLLOW
85 Church St., Burlington, 802-863-6458
One Mill St., Middlebury, 802-388-3177
Rt. 7A, Manchester, 802-362-3321
Fine crafts galleries featuring the work of Vermont artisans.

CREDITS

The authors have made every effort to reach copyright holders of text and owners of illustrations, and wish to thank those individuals and institutions that permitted the reprinting of text or the reproduction of works in their collections. Those credits not listed in the captions are provided below; References are to page numbers; the designations *a, b,* and *c* indicate position of illustrations on pages.

Text

Hayden Carruth: From *Collected Shorter Poems, 1946-1991* by Hayden Carruth. Copyright © 1997 by Copper Canyon Press. Reprinted by permission of the author.

The Culinary Arts Institute: Recipe adapted from *The Fifty States Cookbook* by the Culinary Arts Institute. Copyright © 1977 by Delair Publishing Company, Inc.

Henry Holt & Co., Inc.: "The Pasture," from *The Poetry of Robert Frost,* edited by Edward Connery Lathem. Copyright © 1958, 1962 by Robert Frost. Copyright © 1967, 1970 by Lesley Frost Ballantine. Copyright © 1930, 1939, © 1969 by Henry Holt & Company. From *Green Mountain Verse,* excerpt from "East of Bridgewater" by Ann Batchelder. Copyright © 1943 by Enid Herberta Crawford Pierce.

Houghton Mifflin Co.: Excerpt from "For Robert Frost," from *Flower Herding on Mount Monadnock* by Galway Kinnell. Copyright © 1964 by Galway Kinnell. All rights reserved. "The Falls," from *Three Books,* Copyright © 1993 by Galway Kinnell. Previously published in *Body Rags* (1967). All rights reserved.

Little, Brown & Co.: From *Vermont Tradition: The Biography of an Outlook on Life* by Dorothy Canfield Fisher. Copyright © 1953 by Little, Brown & Co.

Lyons Press: *Walking the Dead Diamond River* by Edward Hoagland. Copyright © 1973 by Lyons Press.

W. W. Norton: From *Vermont: A Bicentennial History* by Charles T. Morissey. Copyright © 1981 by W. W. Norton and the American Assn. for State and Local History, Nashville.

Penguin Putnam Inc.: From *Where the Rivers Flow North* by Howard Frank Mosher. Copyright © 1971, 1972, 1973, 1974, 1978 by Howard Frank Mosher. Used by permission of Viking Penguin, a division of Penguin Putnam Inc.

Random House, Inc.: *Living the Good Life: How to Live Sanely and Simply in a Troubled World* by Helen and Scott Nearing. Copyright © 1970 by Schocken Books.

Norman Rockwell Family Trust: *My Adventures as an Illustrator* by Norman Rockwell. Copyright © 1960 by Bantam Doubleday Dell. Reprinted by permission.

William Jay Smith: "A Minor Ode to the Morgan Horse." Copyright © 1961, 1988 by William Jay Smith. Reprinted by permission of the author.

University Press of New England: Noel Perrin, excerpt from *Amateur Sugar Maker* © 1972 by Noel Perrin.

Illustrations

AMERICAN MUSEUM OF FLY FISHING, MANCHESTER: **86c**; KEN ARTHUR COLLECTION: **15b** *Catamount.* Wood, gilded. 64 x 22". Photo Tad Merrick; BEN & JERRY'S HOMEMADE HOLDINGS, INC.: **66b**; BENNINGTON MUSEUM: **17** Wasp auto, **34a** *Battle of Bennington* Oil on canvas. 13 x 17"; **35a** *Captain Elijah Dewey.* Oil on canvas. 45½ x 34 ¾ "; **50b** *Easter Dawn Mass.* Oil on canvas. 48 x 73¾"; **61b** Clock; **63a** Quilt; BREAD AND PUPPET THEATER/JOHNSON MEMORIAL GALLERY: **76b** *Peace Hand Puppet;* BUFFALO MUSEUM OF SCIENCE: **27b**; CANADIAN MUSEUM OF CIVILIZATION, QUEBEC: **28b** Abenaki headband; CENTER FOR CREATIVE PHOTOGRAPHY, UNIVERSITY OF ARIZONA: **49** *"Nose-Dive Annie";* MR. AND MRS. TED CHAFFEE: **68b** Loon decoy. Wood and paint. 9½ x 17 x 5"; ANN COLEMAN: **71** *Heading North.* Watercolor. 7 x 9"; CORBIS: **69**, **87a** Bob Krist; CURTIS PUBLISHING/ NORMAN ROCKWELL FAMILY TRUST: **46** *Blacksmith's Boy—Heel and Toe.* Oil on canvas. 72 x 35"; DANFORTH PEWTERERS: **62a** Oil lamp; F/STOP PICTURES: **50a, 53a**; SABRA FIELD: **55** *Green Bridge.* Woodcut. 20 x 30"; ROBERT HULL FLEMING MUSEUM, UNIVERSITY OF VERMONT: **67** *Chicken Supper.* Oil on canvas. 36 x 30". Gift of Barbara, Jane, and Stephen Belcher; CHARLES GINNEVER: **85a** *Zeus.* Steel beams. 90' overall; G.R.A.C.E., HARDWICK, VT: **1** *A Beautiful Dream.* Oil on canvas 12 x 16"; **82a** Gayleen Aiken with her Rainbillies. Cardboard cutouts.; FAMILY OF FRANCIS HEWITT: **85b** *Vermont Flag.* Oil on canvas. 36 x 52"; HOLY COW, INC.: **43b** *Grazing.* Serigraph on paper 22½ x 32"; HOOD MUSEUM OF ART, DARTMOUTH COLLEGE: **29b** Birchbark box; LEE HULL: **5** *Gathering Christmas Berries.* Oil on canvas. 31½ x 22¾"; STEPHEN HUNECK GALLERY, WOODSTOCK: **14a** *Brook Trout*; **68a** *Ice Fishing on Lake Willoughby*. Oil on canvas. 20 x 24"; **83b** *Lab Throne*; IMAGEWORKS: **14b**, **48a**, **56**; WOLF KAHN: **2** *Apple Tree Surrounded by Maples*. Oil on canvas. 30 x 40"; **84** *Trees Changing Color*. Oil on canvas. 36 x 52"; KAREN KARNES: **82b** Stoneware bowl; FRANK LARSON: **38** *Indian Summer*. Oil on canvas. 30 x 40"; MERCHANTS BANK, BURLINGTON: **39a** *Logging Camp in Vermont*. Watercolor. 18½ x 11½"; METROPOLITAN MUSEUM OF ART, NEW YORK: **20** *The Belated Party on Mansfield Mountain*. Oil on canvas. 38 x 63⅛". Rogers Fund, 1969; MIDDLEBURY COLLEGE: **75**; MINNEAPOLIS INSTITUTE OF THE ARTS: **22** *Village of Stowe, Vermont*. Oil on canvas. 33½ x 23⅝"; GRANDMA MOSES PROPERTIES CO., NEW YORK: **78a** *Grandma Moses on Her 101st Birthday*. © 1982; **78b** *Christmas at Home*. Oil on pressed wood. 18 x 23". © 1996; **79** *In the Park*. Oil on canvas. 36 x 45". © 1996; **80** *Sugaring Off*. Oil on pressed wood. 23 x 27". © 1991; **81b** *Battle of Bennington*. Oil on pressed wood. 18 x 30½". © 1996; MUSEUM OF AMERICAN FOLK ART: **47a** *Trade Sign*. Painted wood. 84 x 66 x 36"; **58b** Chest; MUSEUM OF FINE ARTS, BOSTON: **44** *A Marble Quarry*. Oil on canvas. 18 x 24". Gift of Maxim Karolik for the M. and M. Karolik Collection of American Paintings, 1815–65; MUSEUM OF FINE ARTS, SPRINGFIELD, MA: **51** *Church Supper*. Oil on canvas 40 x 48". James Philip Gray Collection; NATIONAL GALLERY OF ART: **37b** *Vermont Lawyer*. Oil on canvas. 44 x 35½". Gift of Edgar William and Bernice Chrysler Garbisch. © 1998 Board of Trustees; NATIONAL GEOGRAPHIC IMAGE COLLECTION: **12a** Flag. Illustration by Marilyn Dye Smith; **12b** Thrush and clover. Illustration by Robert E. Hynes; NATIONAL PORTRAIT GALLERY /ART RESOURCE: **57a** *Portrait of Calvin Coolidge*. Etching and drypoint. 7⅛ x 4". NEW BRITAIN MUSEUM OF AMERICAN ART, CT: **19** *A View of Vermont*. Oil on canvas. 26½ x 40". Grace Judd Landers Fund. Photo Michael Agee; NEW YORK STATE HISTORICAL ASSOCIATION: **53b** *The Village Post Office*. Oil on canvas. 36¼ x 47¼"; OLD STONE HOUSE MUSEUM, BENNINGTON: **47b** Chapel organ; HERB PECK COLLECTION: **36b**; PANORAMIC IMAGES: **11**, **27a**, **54b**, PHOTO RESEARCHERS: **15a**; PEACHAM HISTORICAL SOCIETY: **62b** Butter mold; PRIVATE COLLECTION: **37a** *The Haymakers*. Oil on canvas. 30 x 50"; PROCTOR MARBLE EXHIBIT: **13a** Replica of *The Last Supper*. 6 x 12 x 3'; NORMAN ROCKWELL FAMILY TRUST: **60b** *Norman Rockwell Visits a Family Doctor*. Oil on canvas. 32 x 60"; ROKEBY MUSEUM: **26** *Camel's Hump*. Oil on board. 6½ x 7½"; JIM SARDONIS: **45b** *Braintree Panthers*. Braintree pink granite. 3 x 4 x 2'; **87c** *Whales' Tails/Reverence*. African granite. 13 x 20 x 10' overall; CLELAND E. SELBY: **52** *Our Town at Dawn*. Wool and burlap. 3 x 6'; SHELBURNE MUSEUM: **9** *View Along the Connecticut River*. Watercolor on paper. 41½ x 56½"; **10** Cutter; **39b** Plow; **40b** Sugaring scene; **45a**, **59b**, **63b** Basket; **64**; SOUTHERN VERMONT ART CENTER, MANCHESTER: **40** *Sugar House*. Oil on canvas. 40 x 51"; STATUARY HALL COLLECTION, WASHINGTON, D.C.: **32b** *Ethan Allen*. Office of the Architect of the Capitol; TIME LIFE SYNDICATION: **72b** *Alexander Isayevich Solzhenitsyn*; UNIVERSAL PRESS SYNDICATE: **57b** *Doonesbury* © 1981 G. B. Trudeau. All rights reserved; UNIVERSITY OF VERMONT, SPECIAL COLLECTIONS: **29a** Abenaki natives. Engraving; **32a; 70b** Winter Carnival; **74**; VERMONT HISTORICAL SOCIETY, MONTPELIER: **30** Sheet music; **33a** Poster; **33b** *Ruins of Fort Ticonderoga*. Oil on academy board. 33½ x 44½"; **34b** Coin; **42** *Merino Rams*. Engraving. 12¾ x 17⅝"; VERMONT LIFE, INC.: **70a** *Vermont Life* cover; VERMONT SECRETARY OF STATE: **12c** Coat of arms; PACE WILDENSTEIN GALLERY, NEW YORK: **83a** *A Heart Like Mexican Weather*. Oil on canvas. 60 x 42"; WINTERTHUR MUSEUM: **31** *South View of the Fortress and Camp at Crown Point*. Watercolor. 14¼ x 20⅝"; T. W. WOOD GALLERY AND ARTS CENTER, MONTPELIER: **24** *Man in the Woods*. Watercolor. 10 x 13"; **88** *Thomas Waterman Wood*. Self-portrait. Oil on canvas. 30 x 25"

Acknowledgments

Walking Stick Press wishes to thank our project staff: Miriam Lewis, Joanna Lynch, Kina Sullivan, Thérèse Martin, Laurie Donaldson, Lani Gallegos, Nancy Barnes, Mark Woodworth, and Adam Ling. For other assistance with *Vermont*, we are especially grateful to: Nancy Friedman, Laurel Anderson/ Photosynthesis, Lindsay Kefauver/Visual Resources, Paul Carnahan of the Vermont Historical Society, Carol Putnam of the G.R.A.C.E. arts program, Gwen and Stephen Huneck, David Levinthal, Garry Trudeau, Tad Merrick, Jim Sardonis, and the staffs of the University of Vermont/Special Collections, the Shelburne Museum, the Bennington Museum, the Robert Hull Fleming Museum, Middlebury College, the Norman Rockwell Family Trust, *Vermont Life* magazine, and the Vermont Folklife Center.